The Passion to Skate

The SPASSION to SKATE

AN INTIMATE VIEW OF FIGURE SKATING

BY SANDRA BEZIC

WITH DAVID HAYES

Andrews McMeel
Publishing

Kansas City

AN OPUS BOOK

For my mother.
S. B.

www.andrewsmcmeel.com

Library of Congress Cataloging-in-Publication Data

98 99 00 01 RDW 10 9 8 7 6 5 4 3 2

Bezic, Sandra.
      The passion to skate: an intimate view of figure skating / By Sandra Bezic and David Hayes.
          p. cm.
      Includes index.
      ISBN 0-8362- 6452-5 (ppb.)
      1. Skating. 2. Skating—Tournaments. I. Hayes, David, 1953– . II. Title.
GV850.4.B49 1996
796.91'2—dc20   96-28251
                                                        CIP

A hardcover edition of this book was published in 1996 by Turner, Publishing, Inc.

ATTENTION: SCHOOLS AND BUSINESSES
Andrews McMeel books are available at quantity discounts with bulk purchase for educational, business, or sales promotional use. For information, please write to: Special Sales Department, Andrews McMeel Publishing, 4520 Main Street, Kansas City, Missouri 64111.

TABLE OF CONTENTS

A t a time when figure skating is more popular than ever before, Sandra Bezic's The Passion to Skate provides a dramatic, behind-the-scenes glimpse into the world of elite athletes in training, competition, and performance.

Throughout her career as a competitive skater and, later, as a choreographer for many of the world's greatest stars, Sandra has experienced the intense highs and lows of Olympic and World competition. Her respect and affection for the sport make her an appealing storyteller. "After all these years, I still get excited by the potential of skating," she says. "In this book, I wanted to answer the question I've been asked so many times over the years— How do you people do that? In the text and through my choice of photographs, I've tried to capture the movement and show the range of the sport, as well as portray the skaters' personalities."

Engaging and insightful, Sandra recounts the arduous but ultimately rewarding journey top skaters must embark upon to fulfill their dreams. Beginning with her own story, in which a child entranced by the speed and pageantry of skating becomes an Olympic athlete, she relates how she began her career as one of the world's foremost choreographers.

Drawing on her experience as a competitive skater, her gift, she discovered, was integrating artistry with athleticism. Working with Brian Boitano over the months leading up to the 1988 Calgary Olympics, Sandra enabled him to realize his greatness. She details the meticulous, step-by-step creation of a gold-medal-winning strategy. "She creates an environment in which we can experiment with portraying emotions," explains Boitano. "Many times she has inspired me to think about what kind of skater I wanted to be and what I wanted to say as an athlete and an artist."

A skating competition has all the elements of a mythic drama. To perform a complex routine under pressure takes confidence and maturity. To land a triple jump requires building up speed across the ice and hurtling into the air in a blur of barely contained momentum before landing precisely on a quarter-inch edge of tempered steel. The odds against succeeding are enormous, yet entire careers rest on moments like this one. Sandra describes what it takes to compete at an international level, and explores the elusive nature of the competitive spirit. "It takes a tremendous amount of drive, discipline, and heart to become one of the elite skaters," says Sandra. "I'm in awe of them."

FACING PAGE | *Sandra Bezic laughs at Katarina Witt's and Brian Boitano's first efforts at pair skating, in rehearsal for the feature film* Carmen on Ice.

As a choreographer, Sandra finds the music, develops the concept, and designs a program that allows skaters to creatively and gracefully perform their athletic feats. She outlines each of the critical steps in this process, from the sound to the look to the movement. "At times it was like I was going through the motions," says World and Olympic Champion Kristi Yamaguchi, "but then Sandra's special touch brought meaning and inspiration to each move and note of music, no matter how big or small. She gave me the confidence to express more emotion on the ice, and to lose myself in the music and let it carry me through the performance."

Sandra is also co-producer and director of Stars on Ice, one of the most respected and glamorous of the professional skating tours, where she works with stars like Kristi Yamaguchi, Kurt Browning, Katarina Witt, Paul Wylie, and Scott Hamilton to bring their talents to audiences throughout North America. "Skating is a world of very colorful egos," observes Olympic gold medalist Scott Hamilton, who founded Stars on Ice in the mid-eighties. "Sandra has an uncanny ability to pull people together and make them feel at home." Taking us backstage and on the road, Sandra explains the elaborate planning and preparation that go into the creation of a major skating show.

Translating skating onto videotape or film is a different challenge, requiring Sandra to work with elaborate sets or in exotic locations, always taking into consideration how the skaters will appear on camera. Her experiences working on legendary TV specials such as Kurt Browning's You Must Remember This and Brian Boitano's Canvas of Ice, as well as the Emmy-winning feature film Carmen on Ice, starring Katarina Witt, Brian Boitano, and Brian Orser, are brought to life. "She can put together a whole program that works well for the camera, with hand movements, facial gestures, and body language," says veteran producer David Michaels, who has worked on figure skating events for NBC and CBS. "Few can do that. She's unique."

Whether on the competitive circuit, touring with a major ice show, or making a TV program, top skaters are part of a tightly knit extended family. Sergei Grinkov's tragic death while rehearsing with his wife and partner, Ekaterina Gordeeva, for the 1996 Stars on Ice tour shook the family to its foundations. Sandra explains how she and her colleagues dealt with their grief by organizing a tribute to Sergei that embraced and celebrated the entire skating family.

Sandra brushes aside the hoopla surrounding the elite figure skating world. She vividly illustrates the drive, ambition, and passion necessary to transform a dream into a world-caliber reality, revealing her many tricks of the trade with humor and clarity. Referring to her reputation as a personable, gifted, and demanding collaborator, Kurt Browning once said: "Thank you, Sandra, for the migraines and the magic."

Her life and her work revolve around using her prodigious talent to bring together music and movement with skaters, both individually for solo performances and in concert with other creative artists to produce artfully dramatic, athletically ambitious spectacles. It is on this kind of collaboration that she thrives. About her intention in writing The Passion to Skate, Sandra says: "This is my world and these are my friends. This book is about those of us who have chosen to express ourselves through figure skating."

David Hayes

FACING PAGE | Sandra and her collaborator, choreographer Michael Seibert, join creative forces on many varied projects. Here they direct rehearsals for the spectacular, award-winning Carmen on Ice.

CHAPTER 1

THE DREAM

*T*he dream begins the first time you feel your blades cutting across the hard, cold surface and discover the effortless motion of gliding. The first time you find yourself believing, if only for a few moments, that you are the most graceful or the most powerful person in the world. It grows inside you with a surprise discovery: on the ice you are free to express your joy or sadness in movement, jumping or spinning, or simply creating steps entirely your own. Now, in your mind's eye, you can see yourself performing at the Olympics, knowing that all eyes are on you.

You imagine yourself pushing away from the boards, your skates making a sharp, clean hiss like fabric ripping. The lights in the big arena are dazzling, and you hear the buzz of many thousands of spectators drop to sighs and whispers. You stop at center ice, catch a glimpse of a honeycomb wall of camera lenses, and focus on a distant point, patiently waiting for the opening chords of your music. You feel your heart pounding, so you take a deep breath and clear your mind, just as you've practiced doing so many times before. Your dream—no longer mere thoughts, longings, aspirations, goals—comes alive. . . .

Holding your final pose at center ice as the crowd roars its approval, you know you've skated your best. You're out of breath as you glide toward the boards, flushed with exhaustion and emotionally spent. There are the tearful faces of your mom and dad cheering in the stands, and the open arms of your coach, as the little flower girls hand you armloads of bouquets that rain from the sky like praise. Standing on the podium with a gold medal around your neck, you proudly watch your country's flag rise to the stirring sound of your national anthem. This is it, you think to yourself, I did it.

FACING PAGE | *First in line for my debut performance, at the age of three, in a costume made by my aunt. Michael Kirby (right), one of Sonja Henie's partners in the movies.*
RIGHT | *My first publicity photo for a club carnival.*

I can't remember a time when I wasn't able to skate. Mum made sure of this by putting me on the ice for the first time when I was three years old. She was born in northern Ontario in 1927, the year Norway's Sonja Henie won her first World Championship, and a decade later, after the ten-time World Champion and three-time Olympic gold medalist had become a Hollywood star, one of her movies ignited in my mother a passion for skating. The daughter of immigrants from Croatia, Mum was unable to pursue her dream; there just wasn't the extra money for skates or lessons. She collected bottles to pay for a pair of tube skates and to see every skating movie that came through town. To this day, I think she still dreams of being a skater.

Both my parents' families came from the same village on Šolta, a tiny island in the Adriatic Sea south of Split, Croatia. My father, Dusan Bezic, a refugee, had never seen ice before he came to Canada at the age of twenty-five. He met my mother, Angeline Mateljan, while boarding at her parents' home in Toronto. After they became engaged my mother insisted that he learn to skate, and my father, who must have been very much in love, gamely wobbled around the ice a few times. But it wasn't until my older brother Val and I came along that skating became the focus of our family's life.

Every year my parents took us to see *Ice Capades* and *Ice Follies*. Sitting in the front row, I wished the spotlight would hit me because, if it did, if they could just get a glimpse of me, I would surely be asked to put on my skates and perform. Mum and Dad also took us to the ballet, and I remember reading and re-reading a children's book called *The Little Ballerina*, imagining that it was my story. When Mum enrolled me in a children's class at the National Ballet School, I remember the thrill of wearing my own ballet slippers and pink tights with my hair pulled tightly into a bun. Confidently finding a place at the front of the class, I assumed that everyone recognized my dancing gifts.

By the time I was five years old I had decided that I was going to be either a ballerina or a figure skater when I grew up. At home I would wrap one of Mum's scarves around my waist and make up choreography to music on the radio, performing for anyone who would watch. Once I even took my blue bedroom slippers to kindergarten to perform a ballet en pointe. I glided around the living room pretending to skate, and drew pictures of myself standing on the top of an Olympic podium. Always responding instinctively, I discovered a freedom and joy in movement that intoxicated me.

When I was seven Mum decided that our once-a-week skating sessions at the Michael Kirby Skating School were not enough, so she contacted Ellen Burka, one of the country's top coaches. A Dutch National Champion before she came to Canada, Mrs. Burka had coached her daughter, Petra, who, in 1965, would become a World Champion as well as the first woman to land a triple jump. Mrs. Burka was an

LEFT | An unsuspecting cover girl for a national Japanese magazine feature, published shortly after the 1972 Sapporo Olympics.
FACING PAGE | With my brother Val, in 1966, striking a pose borrowed from an Ice Capades program and wearing a dress my mother made that was a replica of a Petra Burka costume.

TOP LEFT | *Unlike North American and European skaters, China's Lu Chen grew up without role models in a country that has almost no history of figure skating. The dream can take root in unlikely soil.*

BOTTOM LEFT | *At nine, Brian Boitano had just begun skating. His longtime coach, Linda Leaver, took the photo.*

RIGHT | *Hard to imagine an eight-year-old Paul Martini, dressed as a caterpillar for a club*

old-school coach whose philosophy was to draw out the best from her skaters through adverse conditioning. I know she felt warmly toward me and believed I was talented, but all the criticism would eventually take its toll.

Everything came easily to me. I won the first competition I ever entered when I was seven, but my second competition, a year later, was significant considering the career I would have much later. I had come in seventh in compulsory figures in an interclub singles event. When I began my free skating program, I got confused because it was a different rink from the one I'd been practicing in. I forgot my program, so instead I began to improvise. I recall vividly the feeling I had as I instinctively moved to the music, jumping and spinning with total abandon. When my music ended, I skated off the ice and burst into tears, telling Mum I had done it all wrong. A few moments later, my girlfriends rushed over to tell me I had won.

My brother Val and I started skating together as a pair in 1965, when he was eleven and I was eight. Both individually and as a pair, we were strong competitors. A year later we qualified at the novice level for our first national competition, which was held in Peterborough, a city a couple of hours drive from Toronto. Our parents made skating a family event. I remember driving there in the morning, competing, then going out for pizza in the evening to celebrate the fact that we'd come in second-to-last instead of last.

The following year, in 1967, we won the same event and there I was, ten years old and granting my first interview. Today, holding the yellowed newspaper clipping that Mum proudly saved, I feel both amused and a little embarrassed at what the reporter wrote. "The little girl with the turquoise bow in her hair looked the interviewer straight in the eye and said: 'I want to compete in the World Figure Skating Championships. And I want to compete in two events at the same meet.' " That hadn't happened at Worlds in twenty years, but I guess I didn't see any reason for it not to happen to me.

Within three years we won our first senior Canadian pair title. Afterwards, Mum sat us down and said: "You've fulfilled every dream I've ever had. If you do nothing more I'd still be happy." But we continued to progress. Because I was only thirteen years old, I required special permission from the International Skating Union (ISU) to compete in the World Championships, which were being held in Ljubljana, Slovenia (at that time part of Yugoslavia). For my father, who had left Croatia as a refugee during the war and was now returning home for the first time, it was an emotional event. He was pleased that his children had won a national title and were representing his adopted country on the world's stage. On the tiny island of Šolta, where many of our relatives still lived, the entire village gathered around the only TV to watch us. Even though we were just a couple of kids competing against the best—including the legendary ten-time World and three-time Olympic Champion Irina Rodnina, who was skating with her first partner, Alexei Ulanov—we proudly placed fourteenth.

In 1972 we went to the Olympics in Sapporo, Japan. Our goal was to make the top ten and we placed ninth. Considering all this traveling part of our education, not just competition for its own sake, our parents made sure we fully experienced the countries we visited. So we stayed in Japan an extra week to visit Kyoto while everyone else rushed home to train for the upcoming Worlds. Mrs. Burka was annoyed, but my parents felt it was important to take advantage of this rare opportunity to see the world.

While Dad was proud of our accomplishments and worked around the clock to support us, Mum was the driving force. With infinite energy she got us up at six in the morning, got us to the rink, and then to school, picked us up after school to return to the rink, and made sure we got to our jazz, ballet, and piano lessons. Many a dreadful winter morning I would sit on my bed while Mum yanked on my tights, only to leave the warmth of our home for a cold car and then a colder rink. She always kept our spirits up and even found time to sew our costumes.

I was absolutely sure that figure skating was going to be my career. I just assumed we'd win everything and then turn professional and join *Ice Capades*. It was the dream shared by so many young figure skaters, and like so many I was a super-achieving kid. A conscientious student, I did my homework during recess and lunch hour, or even when we were at competitions, mailing in reports from all over the world. But I didn't have any kind of social life at school. I remember only a few classmates and even fewer teachers. Life revolved around the next skill that needed to be learned, the next competition, the next event. Looking back, I realize that I never really learned to savor the moment because I was always planning ahead. I was skating before school and after school and on weekends, but I was happy.

Then, when I was seventeen, my whole world fell apart. Val and I had been Canadian pair champions five times, and we'd climbed up the World Championship ladder from fourteenth to fifth. We were the highest-ranking Western pair, preparing ourselves to challenge the Soviets and East Germans, who dominated pair skating at that time. We had even declined an offer from *Ice Capades* because in those days turning professional meant you could never again compete in amateur competitions like the Olympics.

Practicing a throw double-Axel, I injured my ankle, and kept reinjuring it by impatiently returning to the

ice before it had properly healed. Finally, the doctors put a cast on my foot and we had to sit out the rest of the season. It was like hitting the boards. Sitting in the stands at competitions, I began to see only the negative things about skating: the politics, the judging, the enormous pressure my friends were under. I'd watch skaters who had trained for the entire year fall once and lose everything.

All the color in my dream went gray. I was exhausted, burnt out. I'd loved skating, as well as the lifestyle and prestige that came with success. Where I had always accepted my devotion to the sport without questioning it, now I wondered whether or not I even liked it. Skating had become a burden and a responsibility. That single-minded drive that is

'73国際
フィギュアスケート
エキシビション
大会

LEFT | *Months after pairing up in the summer of 1977, fourteen-year-old Barb Underhill and sixteen-year-old Paul Martini begin their competitive career.*

RIGHT | *Val and I returned to Japan for an exhibition tour in 1973. Skating allowed us to see the world.*
FOLLOWING PAGES | *A pair of dreamers: 1988 Olympic Champions Ekaterina Gordeeva and Sergei Grinkov, from the Soviet Union.*

absolutely essential to making it in any sport was no longer a part of me.

My sense of self-esteem had been built entirely around being a competitive figure skater, but my body and emotions were changing, and I was suddenly very aware of the negativism. At twelve or thirteen, when I was criticized for something I had done on the ice, my reaction was to be mentally tough. I would think: *Oh yeah? I'll show you.* At seventeen, I'd started taking what was said to heart. I was a typical teenager going through the kind of self-doubt and frustration that all teenagers go through, except for me there was a lot more at stake. My parents tried to help, but I wouldn't listen. Finally, I decided to quit.

For three years I didn't go to a rink, or watch skating on TV. It's still painful for me to think about this very difficult time. My desire to compete was gone, and while my brother moved on with his life, I tried to figure out my identity *without* skates on. It was inconceivable to me that my life in skating had ended, yet how could I become involved in the sport again? I couldn't imagine myself in a traditional coaching role.

After endless soul-searching, I finally realized that as part of our training Val and I had worked with ballet dancers and modern dance choreographers, but we'd never worked with anyone who was both a professional choreographer and a competitive skater. On a competitive level, choreography is not only about artistry; it is also about designing a program that is structured in a creative way to present the jumps and spins and footwork necessary to winning. Why couldn't I combine my natural gift for working with music and choreography with my experience as an international competitor?

I began by choreographing young kids, novice competitors at local or regional levels, but I felt I would be most effective working at a more elite level. My recent experiences had been at the most senior ranks, and the high stakes of Olympic competition exhilarated me. Within a few months, Louis Stong, one of Canada's top coaches, called me. He had just started working with Barbara Underhill and Paul Martini, who were National Pair Champions. The 1980 Olympics were coming up, and Barb and Paul had all the technical ability but hadn't yet developed a style. Louis, who was busy running his school, didn't want to take full responsibility for them, so he handled their overall strategy and management, and entrusted to me their day-to-day coaching and choreography. Louis and I were partners, but he was also in many ways my teacher, along with his wife, Marijane, an ice-dancing coach. Working closely together for many years, Louis helped me rediscover the joy and satisfaction of the sport.

As someone who had lived the dream almost my entire life, I took my experiences for granted. My crisis taught me how vulnerable and precious dreams are, and I realized how blessed I was to have the ability to express myself through figure skating. I found my way back to the ice, reinventing my dream along the way.

CHAPTER 2

THE   REALIZATION

*M*any skaters dream of standing atop the podium, yet few have what it takes to realize their vision. After years of competing and of helping others to realize their dream, I have seen a lot of performers struggle and fall short—some key element missing from the mix. However, every once in a while a skater appears who completely personifies the dream and who continues to work toward it with unflinching dedication.

Sitting in the stands at the 1987 World Championships in Cincinnati, I watched Brian Boitano lose his title to Brian Orser. Even though it was not Brian Boitano's best performance, I was struck by his precise technique and his physical power. Brian is five-eleven, which is very tall for a free skater, and his choreographic choices seemed to be working against his build. His many small, quick movements looked awkward and mechanical. He was also trying to look into the audience and smile, but he was clearly uncomfortable with this. It was as though someone had said: "You should smile more often." People often dispense this kind of advice in the mistaken belief that big, toothy smiles are the only way to reach an audience. Performers must do what comes naturally to them, and it takes male figure skaters longer than women to find their identities. At that time Brian hadn't found his yet.

To my surprise, Brian's coach, Linda Leaver, who had taught him since he was a child, called me a day or two later and asked me to help him prepare for the 1988 Olympics in Calgary, which were coming up in eleven months. She said she was open to anything, although she asked me to think about keeping his long program music, a collection of classic American tunes. I wasn't convinced that music was right for him, but I respected her opinion. After all, with the Olympics right around the corner it was unheard of to throw everything away and try something new with a former World Champion who's in his prime. Adding to the pressure, the media and the industry would be scrutinizing my every move.

I began by thinking about the big picture. Brian was probably the most majestic skater I had ever seen, and I wanted everyone to recognize that. I also thought about the historic changes that figure skating was going through at that time. Compulsory figures were being phased out, and 1988 would be the last year to include them in Olympic competition. I wanted to make a statement about that as well as what I believed to be Brian's place in the history of the sport. This led me to the music from *Les Patineurs*, a ballet composed by Giacomo Meyerbeer which reflects movements associated with skaters a century ago.

FACING PAGE | *Aware that Brian Orser had earlier skated a sensational short program, Brian Boitano stands waiting for his music, knowing that he cannot afford to make a mistake.*

LEFT | *Linda Leaver, who began teaching Brian when he was nine years old, says of their relationship: "Throughout his career, our hearts and minds were always working toward the same goals. There has always been honesty and trust; there is truth between us."*

RIGHT | *Brian, like all single skaters, practiced school figures four hours a day. A hundred years ago, compulsory figures were the most important part of skating. Over time, their importance gradually diminished and the 1988 Olympics would be the last to include them. This inspired us to use ornate, turn-of-the-century patterns as choreography for Les Patineurs.*

When Brian came to Toronto a month later, in April, we went to the rink and I asked him to skate for me. Standing in an empty arena watching Brian skate is always a breathtaking experience, but this was the first time I shared the ice with him and I was overwhelmed by his power and ability. We began to experiment with some movements, which was my way of getting to know him and understand his natural style. It also helped me overcome my own case of nerves. For a choreographer, beginning a new program is the most frightening thing in the world. There's nothing in front of you except a blank sheet of ice and a skater who's expecting something brilliant from you. Brian was excited to use *Les Patineurs* for his short program, so we went to work.

Brian is almost perfectly consistent because he's so disciplined and exacting. He's the only skater I've met who knows exactly how many feet away from the boards he needs to be to execute a jump, and he'll repeat it the same way every time. If the rink size changes, he adjusts to it. Most skaters are instinctive; Brian is mathematically precise.

It's important for me to find a style of movement or sometimes a particular move that defines a skater's character. I wanted Brian's defining move to highlight the fact that executing even the most difficult maneuver was for him routine, something he could do perfectly every day, every single time. The most difficult maneuver in the short program is the jump combination. It's often the deciding factor in competition and the entire audience waits for it, anxious to see which skaters manage to land it. Brian's combination was a triple Axel into a double loop. I wanted to find a gesture that captured the bravado of a man secure in his reputation as a champion. While gliding along the ice right after his combination, I had him reach down, wipe his blade with his hand, and flick the snow over his shoulder, as if to say, "That jump was a breeze." It played on an image as old as figure skating itself. What does a skater, like Brian, do when he skates? He wipes his blades, and if he's especially confident of his powers he might just toss the snow over his shoulder.

Brian loved it, but I asked myself, *Could he actually compete in the Olympics and do this?* No one else had been so bold. And then I thought: *Why not?*

Once we'd successfully choreographed the short program, Brian and I convinced Linda that we should go ahead with a new long program. Brian needs to know he's done something a million times before he's comfortable putting it in front of an audience, let alone taking it to the Olympics. Even though a drastic change was completely against his character, his enthusiasm showed how far Brian would go to realize his dream. That made me all the more aware of how critical each of our decisions would be. I had to live up to Brian's dedication. He'd been staying at my home and had become part of the family, and we'd found that, off the ice, he is a warm, cheerful guy who would throw together meals with my husband Dino, and tease me about my lack of cooking skills. But he also lived and breathed the Olympics. I never saw a moment, even over the summer, when he chose relaxation over training. I could see in Brian, more clearly than anyone else I'd met, the kind of idealism, drive, and discipline that makes an Olympic Champion. He was *the dream* all grown up.

ABOVE | *As she stood expressionless watching his long program, Linda knew Brian had what she called his "magic feet." During the last ten seconds, though, tears began rolling uncontrollably down her cheeks.*

With her usual perfect timing, my friend Marijane Stong, the ice-dancing coach, brought me the sound-track for the film *Napoleon*, scored by Carmine Coppola. "I think this might be interesting for Brian," she said. "Why don't you listen to it?"

The music's military theme intrigued me, because I'd been thinking about Brian as a romantic hero, as a man with a mission. Brian also responded to the music and the concept, so we set to work. We first had to edit the music, taking ten seconds from here and combining it with ten seconds from there, always conscious of respecting the integrity of the score. The goal was to create four and a half minutes of music that would inspire Brian every time he heard it. We made eighteen edits by the time we were ready to take it to the ice.

Brian's technical requirements also determined the layout of the music. I knew he wanted to open with his trademark "'Tano" triple Lutz followed by his triple Axel combination, so I edited the music to exactly match the number of steps he needed between the two jumps. Every program must be planned to match a skater's cardiovascular capacity. A smaller man can get through a four-and-a-half-minute long program more easily than someone Brian's size. Each spurt of energy was followed by a rest to make sure he was as strong as possible at the end. And because Brian's natural style is large and commanding, I wanted the choreography to be minimal but dramatic.

When I choreograph a program, I rarely begin at the beginning because I must first discover the style of movement appropriate to the character and music. I choose a section of the score that most interests me, often a slow part somewhere in the middle, and begin experimenting. At this time, Brian wasn't contributing. He was a mirror: I would do a step and he would mimic me while I watched him. Step by step, the piece evolved and Brian's natural style emerged.

Conceptually, the program began with Brian as a soldier marching off to war with the resolve and strength to risk everything, followed by a somber ride back from the fields, filled with doubts. The waltz section shows the handsome, romantic hero at the ball, which is then contrasted by the brutality of war. We called the next part of the program "the naked man," reflecting the "true self" under the uniform, vulnerable and exposed. The program came to a close with, of course, the victory march.

These images were not for public consumption; they were to inspire Brian throughout his program. A private man whose strength was with the athletic side of his sport, Brian was less comfortable performing. In essence, we had choreographed Brian's dream, the story of a dedicated athlete's quest to be the best in the world. By giving him a romantic persona that provided a rationale for the movement, he found the freedom to emote, to reveal himself.

At about the three-and-a-half-minute mark in "the naked man" section, we'd wanted to make sure Brian had enough energy for what would be the technical climax of the program: his second triple Axel. We came up with a simple glide on his left leg with his left arm reaching upward. I told him: "If you feel as though you're

ABOVE | *During the last minute of warm-up for his long program, Brian heard his negative voice saying: "You're gonna blow it. You can't do it." Then, as he bent to tighten his skate for the last time, he said to himself: "No, I'm not going to blow it. I can do it. Just take one thing at a time. Stay in the moment."*

too tired, do this and you'll forget about your fatigue. Just think about why you've trained for your entire life and what it is you really want. Reach for every ounce of energy left in your body."

The showcase of the 1988 Olympics was going to be the "Battle of the Brians"—Boitano against Orser. It is the coach's responsibility to map out the schedule and strategy for the season, and Linda was exceptional at this. She understood Brian completely; everything was perfectly calculated to benefit him. She had him debut the new program at Skate Canada in November 1987, not because he'd be competing against Brian Orser, as everyone thought, but to get him into Calgary's Saddledome, where the Olympics were going to be held a few months later. In January, at the U.S. Nationals, he did a brilliant short program and a mediocre long program. But he wasn't challenged by anyone there, so it wasn't the place to be wonderful. Every time he performed, the three of us conferred and then adjusted and fine-tuned, allowing the programs to evolve and grow.

On the day of the short program at the Olympics, I played it very cool and collected around Brian, but inside I was completely wired. Over the past ten months I had witnessed his courage and commitment and deeply believed he deserved to reach his goal. I thought: *The good guy always wins, right?* But then I asked myself: *Who am I to think he's the only good guy?*

Once again, Linda proved herself to be a capable strategist. The short program is worth one-third of the marks, but anyone who places among the top three has an equal chance of winning overall. With Brian already in second place after the compulsory figures, Linda very wisely pulled him back a little, because she didn't want him to burn himself out in his short performance. You can do that with Brian, because just as he knows within an inch where he must be to execute a jump, he also knows precisely what degree of effort is needed to win. I felt frustrated by Linda's decision because I knew how brilliant he could be, but I agreed with her. After placing second to Brian Orser's outstanding performance, Brian was hungry for victory.

Now it was time to give everything he had to the long program. He was pleased with his skating order. Coming first after the six-minute warm-up is not a popular choice among competitors, but Brian felt confident that he could warm up adequately in four or five minutes, then use the final minute to let his heart rate come down before skating his program. There would be enough time to get a feel of the ice, but no chance for doubts or insecurities to take hold. Skating first also meant he skated before Brian Orser, which was to his advantage because he would establish the standard that had to be bettered. Looking back, I truly believe that at this point it was no longer about winning; it was about performing perfectly everything that he had spent a lifetime learning.

When the Olympics are held in North America it's electrifying. For one thing, the venues are huge. In Europe, the arenas hold a few thousand people, and since many are from the media there isn't as much applauding and cheering. Twenty thousand fans packed the Saddledome that February day in 1988, and the excitement over the men's event, with all the hype about the "Battle of the Brians" pitting the American against the Canadian, was reaching its climax.

ABOVE | *Standing at rinkside, where Brian wanted me to be, I thought:* Have I done everything I could for him?
FACING PAGE | *At the emotional climax of the program, Brian lands his second triple Axel.*

"IT'S ALWAYS HARD TO FIND THE RIGHT THING TO SAY TO EACH COMPETITOR JUST BEFORE THEY GO ON THE ICE. THAT EVENING, AFTER REHEARSING ALL SORTS OF LONG-WINDED WORDS OF WISDOM, I SIMPLY SAID TO BRIAN: 'THIS IS YOUR MOMENT. SHOW THEM YOUR SOUL.'"

LEFT | *Every day for a year, Brian visualized this moment— the thunderous ovation, the tears, the laughter, standing on the podium watching the American flag being raised as the national anthem played. Afterwards he told me, "Everything was exactly as I'd imagined, except for one thing: The tempo of* The Star Spangled Banner *was much faster than it had played in my mind."*

RIGHT | *As defending World Champion and the Canadian in Calgary, no one was under more pressure than Brian Orser (left) who performed valiantly to win his second Olympic silver medal. Viktor Petrenko (right), the emerging new star from the Soviet Union, also skated superbly to win the bronze.*

As he quietly paced backstage, Brian was aware that many do not give their best performances when they're under the kind of pressure created by Olympic competition. As we looked into each other's eyes, I knew what he was thinking. Even though he was superbly trained, both mentally and physically, and we both knew he could skate a perfect performance because he'd done it many, many times, he wondered: *Can I do it now?*

It's always hard to find the right thing to say to each competitor just before they go on the ice. That evening, after rehearsing all sorts of long-winded words of wisdom, I simply said to Brian: "This is your moment. Show them your soul."

Standing in my chosen spot, right at rinkside a few feet behind and to the left of Linda, where Brian wanted me, I skated every step as he did. Time seemed to stop and I wasn't even aware of the roaring crowd. Brian was magnificent, jump by jump, move by move. There was no caution in his performance. As I watched him do that glide, his arm reaching up in preparation for his second triple Axel, I knew he wouldn't back down, that he would risk everything and pull in to rotate three-and-a-half times. With a near-perfect landing, he nailed it.

Viktor Petrenko had never skated better than he did that day, and he ended up with the bronze. Brian Orser also skated brilliantly, but he made one small mistake on the triple flip, and probably a more fatal mistake when he decided to turn his second triple Axel into a double. In any other year, in any other competition, Brian Orser would have won with that performance. But I believe that, just as Brian Orser had had the electricity for the short program two nights earlier, on one of the greatest nights of figure skating history, Brian Boitano gave the performance of his life.

FOLLOWING PAGES |
*Brian Boitano executing
a "'Tano" triple Lutz.*

THE COMPETITION

*W*here do elite skaters get the inner strength to compete? How does it feel knowing that the impact of a single performance could fulfill a lifelong dream or shatter it?

Failure is not the only fear. I attended the Helsinki World Championships in 1983 with Barbara Underhill and Paul Martini, who were the top Canadian pair. When Barb said she wanted to talk to me, I assumed she was concerned that she and Paul might fall and blow their shot at a bronze medal. Instead, she asked: "What if we *do* it?" Success can be as frightening as failure, because suddenly skaters must move on to the next level where the pressure to succeed is even greater.

Some people are born with a competitive edge. It seems you either have it or you don't, but is this necessarily so? It's probably the most important question coaches ask themselves when they begin working with new skaters: *Is it possible for me to teach this person how to compete? Is mental strength an ingredient that can be developed?*

Certainly skaters such as Brian Boitano, Kristi Yamaguchi, and Katarina Witt appear to have been born with it. Brian's performance at the 1988 Olympics was the perfect combination of talent, drive, concentration, and training. Part of the training is learning not to listen to critics, not to believe your press clippings, and not to get caught up in hundreds of other distractions. Most important, it's developing the concentration to

simultaneously control your body, mind, and emotions. Skaters call it "making the butterflies fly in formation." When Brian won the gold medal, his satisfaction didn't come from beating his competitors but from overcoming the external and internal forces that threaten to undermine an athlete's spirit. He competed against himself, and triumphed.

I first worked with Kristi when she was sixteen and so shy that she barely spoke to me or my family throughout the time she stayed with us. It took years for quiet, undemanding, and obedient Kristi to learn to challenge my ideas, which is unusual because we expect top athletes to have an ego to match. But Kristi's calm demeanor conceals a drive and an inner strength that has made her the most consistent female skater

TOP | *At the 1996 World Championships in Edmonton, fifteen-year-old Michelle Kwan, the leader after the short program, was the last of the contenders to skate. Her main competitor, defending World Champion Lu Chen, had earlier given a flawless performance.*
BOTTOM | *After a successful short program at the 1992 Albertville Olympics, placing third, Paul Wylie finally realized that he could translate his potential into performance. He thought, I can do this.*

ABOVE | *After winning the silver medal in Albertville, Paul Wylie went on to become one of the most consistent professional skaters today. He told me, "After Albertville, I felt differently about myself and people treated me differently." He was now a champion.*

RIGHT | *Facing the kind of pressure that makes many skaters crumble, Michelle Kwan performed with conviction and won the title.*

ABOVE AND LEFT | *Competing as a professional can be quite an adjustment because entertainment is as important as technical content. Although these events are gaining legitimacy because of the high caliber of skating, some things never change. One of the most magnetic skaters, 1992 Olympic gold medalist Viktor Petrenko demonstrates how to win audiences and influence (some) judges.*

competing today. Over her entire career you can probably count on one hand the number of not-quite-perfect performances.

Katarina Witt has always been one of figure skating's greatest competitors. In Cincinnati in 1987, when Kat was faced with trying to win back her World title from Debi Thomas, she was the final skater after Debi had performed brilliantly and the other women had been almost equally strong. That would have unnerved most skaters, but with her indomitable will Kat took command of the arena. She skated to the music from *West Side Story*, cleanly executing a beautifully integrated program of jumps and intricate choreography. Seductive and filled with self-assurance, Kat defiantly made eye contact with the audience as if to say, "Watch me, I'm going to outperform everyone." To do so under those circumstances took almost superhuman confidence.

Yet Paul Wylie, a fine skater who, early in his career, seemed to lack the psychological toughness necessary to win, somehow acquired it at just the right time. At the 1992 Olympics, Paul was not a front-runner. He'd never won a U.S. title nor been a medal winner in a World Championship. Everyone acknowledged that he was one of the most talented skaters around, but he had been dismissed as a weak competitor. In Albertville, however, he won the silver medal with a performance that many people believe should have earned gold.

Paul told me that knowing 1992 was going to be his last year as an amateur, he couldn't have lived with his final memory being a poor Olympic performance. He had trained so hard for it that he could cleanly execute his long program twice consecutively on a daily basis, which is extraordinary in itself. By over-preparing, he had finally overcome his doubts and convinced himself he could do it. Paul discovered what for him was the secret to competing, and he's never lost it. He's been a successful professional competitor ever since.

It's the psychological outlook as well as the training that sets the champion apart. Successful performers understand themselves completely—their strengths and limitations, goals and fears—and have learned what kinds of rituals and mental tricks work for them. Scott Hamilton will pace backstage saying, "I can't do it, it's not right, I don't have the energy tonight." But that's just his way of facing his demons. He and everyone else around him know that his performance will be up to his usual high standards.

It is the coach's job to create an environment that will set skaters on the road to self-discovery. The luck of the draw determines the order in which each competitor skates, and each position requires a different preparation. If you have drawn first to compete, you must condense the six-minute warm-up to about five minutes so that your heart rate comes down before you begin your performance. Usually the preferred spot is second or third, because you can use the full warm-up while still having enough time to recover before competing. If you're skating sixth and last, you could be waiting up to forty minutes between your warm-up and your performance.

The longer the wait, the harder it is to keep muscles loose and warm. Skaters always loosen or remove their skates. Everyone spends part of the time stretching or running on the spot. Since it's impossible to stay focused for a prolonged period of time, skaters learn how to escape mentally as well as how and when to return their focus to the moment at hand. Some relax themselves by listening to their favorite music on a Walkman; others physically or mentally walk through their programs. A few nervously chatter to their coaches, while others find an isolated corner where they can be alone.

The pressure starts to build from the moment you arrive at the site. For ten days it's like living in a fishbowl: reporters, photographers, and officials are everywhere. Competitors plan their days around the scheduled practices—when to get up, what to eat, when to train off-ice, if and when to nap, and when to go to bed. Although there is a social aspect—most competitors are also friends who often haven't seen each other for months—it's also a solitary experience because everyone is preoccupied with their preparations, reaching deep inside themselves for every ounce of strength and confidence they can muster. Successful competitors learn to enjoy themselves while at the same time blocking out the most distracting elements.

Practice sessions are strategically planned, since they are intended to build confidence and impress the judges, who watch these practices. One consideration is whether to run through your entire program. In the past, the Soviets were famous for not doing complete run-throughs. Instead they practiced short, impressive sections believing this gave the illusion that their programs were more difficult than they really were. North Americans, who are known to be well conditioned, usually skate their entire program from start to finish to allow judges to appreciate its difficulty and to prove their level of fitness.

There is an etiquette at practice sessions. Over the years you develop a built-in radar that lets you sense where the others are going, and the skater whose music is playing has the right-of-way. In Calgary in 1988, however, Katarina Witt, as three-time World Champion and defending Olympic Champion, wrote her own rules. Reporters and photographers were attracted to the playful and sexy skater like bees to honey, and she rarely disappointed them. Although Kat never got in anyone's way, to her competitors' chagrin she placed herself at an end of the rink where the media had gathered and improvised to everyone else's music.

Along with the etiquette, a pecking order is established that is usually determined by ranking. Practice sessions are an opportunity for displays of competitive one-upmanship that can be more exciting to watch than the event itself. I remember seeing a session in the mid-eighties when Brian Boitano, an American, Brian Orser, a Canadian, and Josef Sabovcik, a Czech, flew around the ice challenging each other to land a quadruple jump. With the testosterone pumping, they, along with everyone in the stands, were having great fun.

On the day of competition, the six-minute warm-up before each group of performances is crucially important. The object is no longer to one-up a competitor but to make sure you're mentally and physically prepared for your performance. For pair and dance teams, the warm-up is more complex since the partners may have to accommodate different responses to stress. For example, one partner may need to talk while the other turns silently inward. Most couples warm up together, rehearsing their movements and experiencing comfort in touching one another. Yet the respected ice dancers Jayne Torvill and Christopher Dean often spent their entire

LEFT | *Midori Ito, the 1989 World Champion and 1992 Olympic silver medalist, was the first woman to land a triple Axel in competition. She is considered the greatest jumper in the history of the women's event.*

ABOVE | *It's a wonderful feeling to be part of a team. At the 1992 Albertville Olympics, two of Japan's leading ladies—Midori Ito (middle row, center) and Yuka Sato (second from right), surrounded by teammates and coaches—cheer on fellow Japanese competitors.*

TOP | *Standing with his coach, Doug Leigh, two-time World Champion and Olympic silver medalist Elvis Stojko prepares to skate his short program at the 1996 World Championships in Edmonton. Although Elvis is one of the strongest competitors in the men's event, no one is immune to mistakes. On this day, he fell, finishing seventh.*

BOTTOM | *Elvis knew, no matter how well he skated his long program, he would not be standing on the podium. But that didn't stop him from skating with all his might. After a resolute performance, he finished in fourth place.*

LEFT AND TOP RIGHT | *Like Brian Boitano and Brian Orser before them, Elvis and Todd Eldredge constantly push each other. After two courageous performances at the Edmonton Worlds, Todd won the title.*

BOTTOM RIGHT | *During the week of practice with his coach, Richard Callaghan, Todd built a steady momentum.*

warm-up apart, stretching their muscles and getting a feel of the ice.

As if the usual pressures of competition weren't enough, skaters often face additional stresses. Midori Ito, the first woman to land a triple Axel in competition, was one of the favorites to win the 1992 Olympics in Albertville. But Japan had never produced an Olympic gold medalist, and you could see that this normally relaxed and happy young woman was carrying the entire weight of her country's expectations on her shoulders. Her tension was building throughout the week, so it came as no surprise when she fell apart during her short program. At the same time, reigning World Champion Kristi Yamaguchi didn't have to live up to quite the same expectations because she was young and her goal was to win the 1994 Olympics. After winning the short program, however, with forty-eight hours off before the long program, she had time to realize that her dream could come true ahead of schedule. It's always hardest to maintain momentum when you find yourself the leader, and many have crumbled under this burden. Although Midori redeemed herself with a performance that pulled her up to second place, Kristi's winning gold was proof of her extraordinary competitive abilities.

However, no one has ever faced more pressure than Nancy Kerrigan at the 1994 Olympics in Norway. Nancy was another gifted skater whose performances were extremely inconsistent. After the infamous whack on the knee by a thug acting on behalf of her teammate, Tonya Harding, Nancy began an intensive rehabilitation and training program. With the entire world watching everything she did, she trained harder than she ever had before in her life. Her magnificent performances in both the short and long programs at Lillehammer under such extreme circumstances are among skating's most respected achievements.

That sixteen-year-old Oksana Baiul won the gold medal over Nancy by a five-four split on the judging panel is just one of many historic controversies surrounding judging in competitions. In figure skating, the blend of athleticism and artistry means judging will always be subjective. In the late seventies, around the time I was thinking about getting involved in skating again, one of the things I had to resolve was whether I could bring myself to send vulnerable young skaters out on the ice to be judged. To skaters, meeting the challenge is more important than the result. At the end of a competition, we all know who won, even if the judging doesn't reflect it. We also believe that everyone who rises to the occasion is a winner, but nonetheless my skaters would have to face formal judging. When I really thought about the results of competitions, I satisfied myself that even though politics and biases will always exist, the International Skating Union (ISU) was doing its best to make judging fair, and that usually the most deserving competitor wins.

At the 1993 World Championships in Prague, a year before the Lillehammer Olympics, I watched Oksana, who a month earlier had come out of nowhere to place second at the European Championships, win the title. She was so gifted athletically and artistically that I said to Dick Enberg, my NBC co-host, "Every once in a while a diamond falls into the lap of the skating world." That an unknown like Oksana can win a World Championship because she deserved it reaffirmed my faith in judging.

"EVERY ONCE IN A WHILE A DIAMOND FALLS INTO THE LAP OF THE SKATING WORLD."
Sandra Bezic talking to NBC co-host Dick Enberg, about Oksana Baiul.

LEFT | *A diva by nature. Upon the announcement of her name, rather than skating to her starting position like anyone else would, Oksana Baiul keeps everyone waiting, then glides in a huge circle until "my feet tell me it's time."*

RIGHT | *Oksana won the first World Championship she ever entered, and a year-and-a-half later became an Olympic gold medalist. This meteoric rise left no doubt about her extraordinary talent.*

| *The pressure of competition can get to even the best. When Katarina Witt stepped into the glaring lights to skate her long program at the 1988 Calgary Olympics, everyone thought her exaggerated makeup was for her character*

Carmen. Afterwards, when she saw footage of herself, she was shocked and embarrassed by her appearance. She said: "I was so nervous in the dressing room that all I could do was apply and reapply my makeup."

| *Elizabeth Manley had a career filled with injuries and illness until her historic perfor- mance in Calgary earned her an Olympic silver medal. She savors the moment, standing with CTV analyst and World bronze medalist, the late Brian Pockar*

Probably my most remarkable competitive challenge occurred in 1984 when Louis Stong and I were working with Canadian pair champions Barbara Underhill and Paul Martini. Barb and Paul are a study in contrasts. Where Barb is intuitive and highly emotional, Paul is methodical and reserved. Together they balanced each other, and by the time they competed at the Sarajevo Olympics in 1984 the four of us had formed a tight bond.

Barb and Paul were expected to win a medal in Sarajevo, and they had a realistic shot at gold. But Barb's injured ankle had kept them out of competition that season and their practices were going poorly. The night before their short program I held a sobbing Barb's hand while a doctor injected cortisone into her foot. During her performance the next day, a fluke fall on a relatively simple spin—caused not by the injury but by a split-second loss of concentration—knocked them out of contention.

With the World Championships a month away, neither Louis nor I was sure whether Barb and Paul would make it. The disaster at the Olympics had shattered their dreams and dealt a potentially fatal blow to their psyches. Even though pair skaters learn not to blame themselves or each other for mishaps, it was impossible not to expect Paul to feel some resentment toward Barb, and for Barb not to blame herself. Their relationship had broken down to the point where they could barely speak to each other. They had experienced an emotional setback so severe that they had lost their confidence; suddenly they were wrestling with the most difficult question of their careers: to quit or face the Worlds in Ottawa and try to redeem themselves. All Louis and I could do was be there for them every day, encouraging them and trying not to show our own sinking hopes.

A week before we were scheduled to depart for the Worlds, just as the four of us were on the verge of canceling, Barb and Paul were sitting in the dressing room with Brian Orser. After listening to Barb complain, Brian said: "Well, why don't you try putting on your old skates?" When she did, it was as though she had set aside all of her problems. That evening she and Paul cleanly skated their long program, and Louis and I could see the old magic had miraculously returned. How much of their recovery was purely psychology? All we knew was that, whether or not they could win it, it was important for them to compete in the Worlds.

During their week-long practice sessions in Ottawa, we could sense a momentum building. On the night of the long program, the mood in the Ottawa Civic Centre, which is an intimate venue for skating, was electric. The crowd knew about Barb and Paul's tragic setback, and sensed that victory was within reach. They were in second place, and as they started to skate they moved decisively, with the confidence of champions. For the final forty-five seconds of their performance the crowd was on its feet creating a deafening roar. Standing in a corner of the building, I jumped up and down and screamed along with everyone else, except I was screaming, "Keep thinking! Keep thinking!" At the end, as flowers were thrown to the ice, Barb and Paul collapsed into each other's arms in relief as much as in victory.

Some skaters are born with a competitive edge and some are able, unexpectedly, to acquire it. Here were two people who had it and lost it, and not only found the strength to regain it but grew stronger from the experience.

ABOVE | *After landing their throw double-Axel (above left), Barb and Paul had completed the last of their most difficult elements. With ten seconds remaining (facing page) they knew they had done it. Having accomplished one of the most dramatic comebacks in skating history (above right), Paul* said: *"As I hugged Barb, savoring the moment, I felt a huge sense of relief that it had worked out after all." Barb said: "We felt we had let everyone down at the Olympics. To have skated so well here, in front of the people we care about the most in our own home country couldn't have been more wonderful."*

FOLLOWING PAGES | *In 1991, Kristi Yamaguchi won her first World title at the age of nineteen. She has become one of the most respected competitors today.*

T H E   S O U N D

*R*avel's *Bolero* has become the signature piece of the great British ice dancers Jayne Torvill and Christopher Dean. Beethoven's *Moonlight Sonata* will always belong to Ekaterina Gordeeva and Sergei Grinkov. Bizet's *Carmen* immediately brings to mind Katarina Witt. *As Time Goes By,* the love theme from the film *Casablanca,* became Kurt Browning's trademark. Each of these examples represents a perfect marriage of skaters, choreography, and music, with the music being the right choice for the right skater, at the right time. I would never ask another skater to live up to one of these classics.

For skaters, music is everything. It is an extension of their personalities, an expression of their souls. At the end of every season, the first question skaters ask is, *What do I want to skate to next?* Choosing the right piece of music is always the most difficult and most important part of my work.

In 1992, three-time World Champion Kurt Browning lost his momentum because of a chronic back injury and placed a devastating seventh at the Olympics. In order to motivate himself with a fresh approach, he moved from Edmonton to Toronto to work with Louis Stong and me. The goal was straightforward: Kurt wanted to win back his World title in 1993. Louis and I felt that for Kurt to accomplish this, along with physical rehabilitation, his new programs would have to make an impact. We felt strongly that to reclaim his position he had to be radically different. We also recognized in Kurt an extraordinary versatility and an ability to affect an audience with his performance.

FACING PAGE AND ABOVE |
At the 1984 Olympics in Sarajevo, Jayne Torvill and Christopher Dean performed their historic free dance to Ravel's Bolero, *for which they received perfect marks.*

One day, Louis's wife, Marijane, whose instinct for matching skaters with music is exceptional, told us she thought Kurt looked a little like Humphrey Bogart and gave us Max Steiner's score for the film *Casablanca.* It was perfect for Kurt's long program. The music had the right elements for skating, and the story behind it would highlight Kurt's ability to portray a character. In fact, I couldn't imagine anyone else being able to do justice to this music. For Kurt, landing the first quad in competition and perfecting triple–triple jump combinations had satisfied his athletic ambitions. The concept of "Casablanca" excited him because he would be able to treat it as a theatrical piece rather than just a competitive program, thereby renewing his love of skating.

The theme revolved around the melody of Herman Hupfeld's song *As Time Goes By,* with its memorable lyrics, "You must remember this, a kiss is still a kiss. . . ." I wanted to capture the internal struggle of a guy in

love forced to make a choice between the woman he loved and doing the right thing. To do that, I had to find the emotional structure for the choreography, and that would be accomplished through editing the music.

Before going into the studio to edit digitally on computer with my friend and music director Marvin Dolgay, I did a rough draft by cutting and pasting on my reel-to-reel tape recorder. The music tells me what to do. As I edit, listening closely and thinking, I begin to understand what the basic attitude of the movement should be. I don't need to get up and move around or go to a rink. I spend far more time working with the music than doing the choreography with the skater. It took about twenty hours to map out the "Casablanca" music, and about half that to pull together the choreography with Kurt.

The one major problem with the music from *Casablanca* was that it had no ending. On the compact disc, it simply faded away. Just a few years ago we would have had to edit an ending from a different recording— or even a different piece of music—and hope it wasn't too noticeable, or scrap the *Casablanca* music altogether. Instead, Marvin composed and recorded an ending that not only gave us the drama I was looking for, but also perfectly matched the existing score. Then, combining his great talent with a sophisticated computer program, he grafted the new passage onto the end of the original score.

Finding the right music from a universe of possibilities, coming up with an idea that suits the skater, and then constructing the music around that idea is the most difficult part of the job. It means editing music for technical as well as artistic reasons. To satisfy judging requirements, coaches and choreographers design programs so that skaters can execute their required elements in the time allowed. In competitive situations, the music score as well as the choreography is built around cardiovascular considerations as much as artistry.

For the short program, I suggested to Louis and Kurt that we find something percussive to contrast with the music from *Casablanca*. After an exhaustive search, Louis came up with Led Zeppelin's *Bonzo's Montreaux*, which turned out to be one of the most challenging editing jobs of my career. I had to turn a four-minute drum solo into a two-minute-and-forty-second short program, editing the piece around Kurt's jumps so they happened in the silences between drumbeats while ensuring that the overall number worked for all eight required elements. A drum solo like *Bonzo's Montreaux* has no melody and few recognizable touchstones like verses and choruses, just pounding drums. It was a perfect vehicle for Kurt, but all I remember is sitting on the floor, surrounded by my razor blade and mounds of cut-up tape, feeling utterly confused and shell-shocked by these drums pounding in my ears for hours. When I finally finished my rough edit, Marvin came to the rescue with his musical knowledge and technical expertise to make sense of what I'd done.

Whether it's Tchaikovsky or some offbeat contemporary number, the music has to make sense physically, emotionally, and competitively. Does the skater love it? Will the audience in the arena and the judges understand it? Will the television audience at home get it? Will it reach them and move them? Many programs don't work because the music functions only as background Muzak, or because the skater doesn't relate to it, or the

FACING PAGE | *On the most emotional swell in the music used for his program, "Casablanca," Kurt Browning captures the spirit of a man in love.*

choreography isn't in tune with the music. Sometimes several pieces of music are combined that don't work together, or they are badly edited. It's important to stay as true to the composer's original composition as possible. With the technology available in recording studios today, tempos can be altered or notes compressed to make the music fit the needs of the program, but when you close your eyes and listen to the end result, it must be musically sound and emotionally satisfying.

I didn't know Lu Chen when I was asked to create both her short and long programs for her 1996 season. Lulu, as her friends call her, had left her home in China at thirteen to train in the United States. Not only could she not speak English, but she had also left behind her family, circle of friends, and culture to follow her dream. Lulu is a very lyrical and feminine skater. She moves her arms beautifully, and has a magical way of tilting her head. Now that she was nearly eighteen, my objective was to find music that would project her beauty and femininity. It was a critical time for her because she was China's first Olympic-level skater, and she was going to be defending her World title.

Whenever I'm looking for music I go to music stores and graze through the racks, reading liner notes and letting my instincts guide me. It's a big guessing game based on my experience listening to a lot of music and learning which labels, orchestras, and conductors are the most promising. In the end I buy thirty to forty compact discs and start listening. Thinking of Lulu, I'd found a collection of traditional Chinese melodies arranged for Western instruments, which I ended up listening to on a summer afternoon on the deck of my cottage. While watching the waves on the water and listening to the wind in the trees, one track caught my attention— a beautiful piece called *Spring Breeze*. It was an unusual choice for a competitive program because it was very delicate and sparse—only violin and guitar—but I decided to present it to her anyway for her short program.

On our first day together, I nervously played it for her, saying that I imagined the movements would be fluid and soft, like a flower or tree swaying in the wind. "I love it," Lulu said with a broad smile, already imagining herself on the ice.

Lulu was staying with me for only two weeks, but in that time I noticed how much she missed family life. She gravitated toward my one-year-old son who adopted her as his favorite babysitter, calling her "Woo-Woo." At the rink, he would holler, "Skate, Woo-Woo," and she would carry him around in her arms. She was warm and gracious, everything her skating had suggested to me.

For her long program, we were again looking for something utterly feminine like *Spring Breeze,* but with more dramatic power. We listened to stacks and stacks of CDs before choosing Rachmaninoff's Piano Concerto no. 2, op. 18, which posed some challenges. For one thing, it slowly and quietly faded out at the end, which is not a safe choice because both judges and audiences tend to like energetic endings. Also, it required several tricky edits. If the music is poorly edited it can end up sounding choppy, the melody can get lost, or you can end up losing the heart and soul of the piece, which is what attracted you to it in the first place. With Marvin's help,

FACING PAGE | *China's Lu Chen taking the final pose of her long program after skating a flawless performance at the 1996 World Championships in Edmonton. She received two perfect 6.0s for presentation, confirming that Rachmaninoff's Piano Concerto no. 2 underscored her grace and femininity.*

we overcame these problems, and when the choreography was finished, Lulu said, "I've never felt so beautiful."

What kind of music works best? I don't believe there are many limitations. The stereotypical skating music is classical, which in many ways seems to lend itself best to movement on ice, although more and more pop music is being used. Generally, the music for competitive situations—not only for the actual performance, but also for the day-to-day rehearsals—has to be inspiring. Some music is so powerfully dramatic that it's almost frightening, and can unnerve a skater in what is already a stressful situation. For example, Mussorgsky's *Night on Bald Mountain* or Leonard Bernstein's symphonic suite from *On the Waterfront* are so intense that they can create a kind of negative energy. But in the right hands I believe anything can work. In 1995, Paul Wylie and his choreographer, Mary Scotvold, recognized that they could use the dynamics in *On the Waterfront* to Paul's advantage, and together they created an affecting program.

Sometimes it's important to be on the cutting edge, particularly for professionals whose most important mandate is to reach an audience. My colleague, Michael Seibert, has a keen sense of what is current in contemporary culture. At a time when seventies funk was becoming big in urban dance clubs, Michael chose *Brick House* by The Commodores for one of Kurt Browning's programs. It was a great success both as a competitive and a commercial vehicle. So was Kristi Yamaguchi's program to *It's Oh So Quiet* by Björk, who is a very hip alternative-pop singer from Iceland, and not someone whose material you would normally associate with figure skating. It worked in part because Kristi's skating, choreographed by Michael, was outstanding and because it introduced Kristi's comic and dramatic talents. But it also worked because Björk was doing a kind of subversive Broadway spoof. The general public, thinking it was a nice show tune, enjoyed it, and the kids in the audience, who recognized Björk from the pop music subculture, thought it was cool.

But often it's still a classical piece that's absolutely right for a skater. Of all the programs I've done for Kristi, my favorite was to Chopin's *Fantasy Impromptu*. I'd first thought of it when Kristi was still an amateur. I knew it was right for her, but it was a delicate piano solo that faded slowly at the end, so I put it aside, waiting for the right time. At the first opportunity, when she turned professional in 1993, we used it to create a long program for a professional competition.

With *Fantasy Impromptu*, the music and the skating were pure. Marvin and I did only one or two edits, so audiences heard Chopin's lovely composition almost unaltered. There was an added dimension to the music as well. *Fantasy Impromptu* had been adapted into *I'm Always Chasing Rainbows,* a popular song by Jane Olivor. I didn't use the vocal version, but the melody was familiar to most of her audience, and the message of the song captured Kristi's spirit, expressing what was in her heart. Kristi has competed with it only three times, and every time she's skated perfectly despite the technical difficulty of the program. I'm always searching for the right music for the right skater; in this case I believe the combination was magical.

"FOR SKATERS, MUSIC IS EVERY-
THING. IT IS AN EXTENSION OF
THEIR PERSONALITIES, AN
EXPRESSION OF THEIR SOULS."

FACING PAGE | *Bizet must have had Katarina Witt in mind when he wrote* Carmen.

FACING PAGE AND ABOVE | *Two progressive musical choices: Kristi Yamaguchi's comedic* It's Oh So Quiet *by alternative pop artist Björk, and Kurt Browning's* Brick House, *a retro-funk number.*

FOLLOWING PAGES | *An all-American boy chooses all-American music: Paul Wylie skating to the soundtrack from the film* JFK.

CHAPTER 5

THE MOVEMENT

*A*fter years of skating, I still get a visceral rush every time I step onto the ice. Whenever I need a fix and I'm working with Barb Underhill and Paul Martini, I ask Paul to do a death spiral with me. Part of the joy of skating is the physicality of the sport. Watching Elvis Stojko reminds me of how satisfying good jumping technique can be. I don't know a skater who doesn't watch with envy Elvis's pure raw energy when he executes a quad. The same is true of Midori Ito's triple Axel, which is bigger and better than most men's. To watch Paul Wylie's incredible speed as he tears around the ice is awesome. And when Lloyd Eisler flips and throws Isabelle Brasseur, their athleticism is a form of daredevil entertainment.

Pure skating technique can be a goal unto itself. It takes great skill and years of training to master our vocabulary of edges and turns. The next step: to marshal all that technique into self expression. For me, the quintessential skater's skater was five-time U.S. Champion Janet Lynn, whose jumps, spins, and footwork, all executed with power and speed, were impeccable. But Janet transcended technique. With a beatific expression on her face, her movements gentle and ethereal, she exposed her soul. If an angel could skate, she would move like Janet.

The possibilities for movement on ice are endless. You can do anything, express anything, be anyone,

and take inspiration from virtually anywhere. For some skaters the joy is in flight; others, like Gary Beacom, are most impressive when their feet don't leave the ice at all. A misunderstood renegade as an amateur, Gary has thrived as a professional. He choreographs himself, and has created wry and brilliantly comic programs.

Where Gary's motivation is primarily to please himself, Scott Hamilton's goal is to please an audience. Working with his choreographer, Sarah Kawahara, Scott has directed his technical skill and gregarious personality toward programs that are extraordinarily detailed, fast and furious, and, above all, entertaining. As a result, twelve years after winning the Olympics, he is arguably the most popular skater on the ice.

Working with a partner offers even more of a range of possibilities,

ABOVE | *Despite the restrictions, World bronze medalists Shae-Lynn Bourne and Victor Kraatz, from Canada, are producing original and refreshing work in the dance event, following in the footsteps of Olympic Bronze medalists Tracy Wilson and Robert McCall.*

FACING PAGE | *Olympic silver medalists Elena Bechke and Denis Petrov demonstrate strength, trust, and timing in performance with Stars on Ice.*

not only dictated by a couple's physical makeup, but also by their emotional relationship. A brother and sister will move differently than lovers, or a divorced couple, or friends. With Barb Underhill and Paul Martini, who are friends, we have taken advantage of their magnetic energy to create a raw, sexual tension. Although Maia Usova and Alexander Zhulin's turbulent marriage may not have affected their choreography, it often affected their performances. Ekaterina Gordeeva and Sergei Grinkov's style was classical and elegant, but their deep and profound love for each other took the quality of their skating beyond the precision of their technique and the perfection of their line. Every action—whether taking each other's hands or glancing into each other's eyes—was filled with such respect, tenderness, and trust that it created an impression of inevitability. To watch them was to watch figure skating at its most sublime.

As a choreographer, it's my job to understand the personality of each individual skater in order to produce an original program. I draw inspiration from the people I collaborate with and from life around me, but I also look inward to find what I have to say and how I can translate that into movement. As with all choreographers, every piece that I create is a reflection of myself as much as it's a vehicle for the skater.

Although a skater's personality and goals have motivated the choice of music, it is listening to the music over and over that inspires the movement and allows me to develop a concept for the choreography. Once on the ice, sometimes the ideas come quickly, as though by magic, but the usual process is a slow discovery, movement by movement. Often I get stuck on as little as four counts of music. When I do, I'll either put it aside and return to it later, go back to the original concept to remind myself of where I'd started, or throw it out and begin again.

Sometimes even the simplest movement can capture the essence of a skater. At one point in Lu Chen's 1996 long program, after an orchestrated passage in Rachmaninoff's Piano Concerto no. 2, op. 18, I heard a rest before a powerfully dramatic piano chord. I asked her to stop and move her arms in an unveiling motion. It was an opportunity for her to reveal something of her heart and soul at this time in her life, to show that she's no longer a little girl. To help her understand, I told her to imagine that she was taking off her robe and letting it drop to the ground, which made us both giggle. *That* gave her something to think about.

Kurt Browning's 1993 long program is a good example of how the smallest details can be the most important. Listening to the musical centerpiece of "Casablanca," the love theme, I imagined this Bogie-like character—a composite of Kurt, my husband Dino, and those cool, tough guys with the soft hearts who epitomized the romantic, 1940s Hollywood notion of masculinity—alone in a bar thinking about the woman he loved and a painful choice he had to make.

I work with Kurt the same way I work with most skaters. Once Kurt and I got on the ice, we played the music over and over, and I did just what I did when I was a child: I started moving to the music, reacting instinctively to whatever felt right. Kurt would watch me, then he would move and I would watch him, and

FACING PAGE | *This is Lu Chen's favorite photo of her 1996 long program because it captures the moment her imaginary robe has fallen to the ice.*

FOLLOWING PAGES | *Moves like the bounce spin are not allowed in Olympic competition because they're considered too acrobatic. As professionals performing with fewer restrictions, 1993 World Champions Isabelle Brasseur and Lloyd Eisler have developed a vast repertoire of spectacular lifts and spins.*

we'd go back and forth, building on each other's steps. It's often wordless communication.

Kurt can be exasperating to work with because he's so gifted that he will invent a brilliant step, and then be unable to repeat it. I have to be particularly alert because I often have to teach him what he's just done. Our roles are clear. He's the incorrigible but charming pupil, and I'm the demanding teacher who has to constantly challenge him. Together, we've done some of our best work.

We agreed that Kurt's Bogie wouldn't do any big, overly flamboyant moves. Bogie was a guy whose heart was tearing up, but he'd never show it. There was a point in the music that I knew was the most important emotional moment. It led into the love theme where I visualized Bogie alone. What would this guy do? After much experimentation, we decided that Bogie flicking away his cigarette said everything about this cool character and his contemplative state of mind. Kurt and I analyzed how someone like Bogie would do that gesture, the movement into it as well as out of it, because there's a difference between the way Europeans and Americans flick their cigarettes.

I had already edited the music so the first two minutes of the program would be filled with energetic skating, and the audience and the judges would be ready for something different, ready for a cigarette break. I couldn't have done that with everyone, but I knew that Kurt has the cardiovascular capacity to handle an intense, two-minute workout, and the theatrical ability to convey the emotion behind such a subtle gesture. To me, that flick of a cigarette was the defining moment, the key that I needed in order to work out the rest of the program.

It was very clear to me that Bogie would never raise his arms above his shoulders. He'd be wearing a white dinner jacket, and he'd make that distinctive movement guys make when they're wearing a suit and they adjust their cuffs. My husband always does it, and it's a very cool, subtle shrug. As we tried to figure out how Bogie would move on the ice, Kurt and I developed a heel-and-toe strut with his hands in his pockets that captured it. The most exciting part of the process was to see how Kurt brought the character to life in performance, adding his own nuances to it. He went on to regain his National and World titles, but the Bogie character took on a life of its own that carried into Kurt's professional career.

In the new world of professional skating, top skaters enter so many competitions that they are obligated to come up with four or five new programs each year. Their schedules mean they're rarely in one place for very long, but somehow the work still has to get done. In the summer of 1994, Kristi Yamaguchi wanted to use a high-energy techno song called *Doop Doop,* by Dancelife Orchestra, for her short program. I thought it was a great idea because Kristi is one of the few skaters who can truly dance. After Marvin and I edited her music, we sent the tape to Kristi, who was training with her coach, Christy Kjarsgaard Ness, in Edmonton. There, they mapped out where each element was to go. Because of the nature of the music, I felt it was important that Kristi work with a contemporary dance choreographer. When Kristi returned to San Francisco, where she lives, I arranged for Barry Lather, a choreographer in California who's done work for Janet and Michael Jackson and

ABOVE | *In empty arenas, while we choreographed his 1993 long program, "Casablanca," I watched Kurt Browning achieve what I thought were moments of genius. I wondered if he would ever be able to skate in performance every little detail we had discussed. The first time he competed with the program was to regain his Canadian title. Not only did he remember all the subtleties of the character, he also managed to add his own flirtatious touches that somehow made Bogie modern. Two months later, the world*

FOLLOWING PAGES | *Jayne Torvill and Christopher Dean have been skating together for twenty years. Over that time, they have experimented with a broad range of styles and movement, and it's exciting to anticipate what they'll come up with next.*

ABOVE AND RIGHT | *One of the reasons Torvill and Dean are the greatest ice dancers in history is because of their work ethic, both on the ice and in the dance studio. The way they've learned to move their bodies, as well as their exceptionally strong skating technique, has given them the tools to express themselves.*

Prince, to meet with Kristi to create funky steps and movements for her. Later in the summer, after a few exhibitions and personal appearances, Kristi finally arrived in Toronto. She had the program's structure mapped out and had learned Barry's quirky dance steps, but now it was up to me to pull it all together.

I had to integrate the technical content with this style of movement. Why would this hip chick who's out dancing suddenly do a boring and very traditional spiral? We had no choice, because the spiral is one of the eight required elements. I asked myself, what would this girl be likely to do if rules forced her to do a spiral that snakes from one end of the rink to the other? I had Kristi get into position, but I also had her put her hand to her chin and impatiently drum her fingers on her cheek, occasionally checking her watch as if to say: "Is it over yet?" Competitive choreography is often about finding ways to do things differently within the confines of the rules.

Nowhere is this more evident than in the dance event. Jayne Torvill and Christopher Dean revolutionized ice dancing with their innovative and complex choreography. At the 1984 Olympics, they broke tradition by skating to Ravel's *Bolero,* which had none of the required tempo changes, and they further pushed ice dancing conventions by spending too much time on their knees and subverting the absurdly detailed lifting restrictions. Although they were rewarded with perfect marks, by the time they turned professional later that year the ISU began tightening the rules.

Meanwhile, the leading Russian dance couples, Klimova and Ponomarenko, and Usova and Zhulin, as well as Isabelle and Paul Duchesnay, skating for France, were strongly influenced by classical and modern ballet, both in their choice of music and their range of movement. As their programs grew more abstract, and their work influenced the rest of their competitors, dancing became increasingly difficult to judge. In order to maintain control and clarify judging, the ISU scrambled to add more and more restrictions, allowing only music with a discernible beat, and movement relating only to ballroom dancing.

Today, what had become figure skating's most creative event has been set back twenty years. The challenge for creative talent, like Canada's Shae-Lynn Bourne and Victor Kraatz, is to find originality and individuality while conforming to ice dancing's limitations.

When you're young, it's human nature to want to go faster, jump higher, and execute more rotations. But the importance of movement and choreography as a means of self-expression increases as skaters age.

Today, Olympic-level skating is thought of as a young person's game. In 1994, however, the year that the ISU allowed previously ineligible professionals to qualify for the Olympics, Katarina Witt surprised everyone by deciding to compete even though she was twenty-eight and couldn't hope to outjump young women like Oksana Baiul or Nancy Kerrigan. Instead, Kat decided to concentrate on her artistry. She brought me an original arrangement of the folk song *Where Have All the Flowers Gone,* saying she had in mind a tribute to the people of war-torn Sarajevo, where she had won her first Olympic gold medal a decade earlier. We concentrated on

ABOVE | *Ekaterina Gordeeva and Sergei Grinkov.*

"EVERY ACTION—WHETHER TAKING EACH OTHER'S HANDS OR GLANCING INTO EACH OTHER'S EYES—WAS FILLED WITH SUCH RESPECT, TENDERNESS, AND TRUST THAT IT CREATED AN IMPRESSION OF INEVITABILITY."

Sandra Bezic, on Ekaterina Gordeeva and Sergei Grinkov

After years of working with the same person, verbal communication becomes unnecessary. The best partners can sense each other's every move and know exactly where to reach to find a hand. The dynamics of the relationship are critical because if there is tension, timing and rhythm are thrown off. Learning to work together is a skill unto itself.

LEFT | Gold, silver, and bronze Olympic medalists and three-time World Champions Marina Klimova and Sergei Ponomarenko.

TOP RIGHT | Gold and silver Olympic medalists and two-time World Champions Natalia Mishkuteniok and Artur Dmitriev.

BOTTOM RIGHT | Olympic silver and bronze medalists and 1993 World Champions Maia Usova and Alexander Zhulin.

ABOVE | *Maia Usova and Alexander Zhulin display the sensuous, dramatic quality they are known for.*
LEFT | *1991 World Champions Isabelle and Paul Duchesnay.*

movements that were melancholic (a graceful picking up and letting go, as though scooping up a bouquet of flowers and dropping them on a grave), maternal (cradling motions), and hopeful (a slow progression up the ice that represented a feminine statement for peace).

Kat didn't win a medal, but her performance deeply moved the audience, the critics, and her fellow skaters. She proved that there is a place in the Olympics for an artistic statement to be made by a mature competitor.

As performers mature, work with their choreographers becomes more and more collaborative. My longest ongoing relationship has been with Barb Underhill and Paul Martini. Over the past sixteen years we've grown up together, and I've always looked forward to meeting them at the rink—to the challenge of artistically renewing ourselves when it feels as though there's nothing new left to be done, to the laughter when we find ourselves all tangled up, our hands in compromising positions.

We've created dozens of programs together, but my happiest experience was choreographing Luba's hit version of Percy Sledge's *When a Man Loves a Woman,* when we had the luxury of the entire summer to experiment without the pressure of a deadline. Barb fits so nicely under Paul when they're facing the same direction. It's cozy, but there's also a real sexiness about it. That's where everything started. As they began to sway, I imagined them

as a couple at a local bar dancing dirty.

Barb and I decided to take advantage of Paul's hunkiness. The movements included a lot of exaggerated teasing and groping. Being a good sport, a red-faced Paul stood still as Barb and I had great fun trying to figure out the best way to grab his butt.

"No, Barb, do it this way."

"No, Sandra, *this* way."

See, part of the joy is the physicality of the sport.

FACING PAGE AND RIGHT |
When Barb Underhill and
Paul Martini step on the ice
together, they exude heat.
FOLLOWING PAGES |
Elena Bechke and Denis
Petrov performing a classic
pair move—the death
spiral—to Samson and
Delilah *during a* Stars
on Ice *tour.*

T H E   L O O K

M any people associate figure skating with sequins and beads. That image certainly captured my imagination as a child, but too often costumes cross the line into bad taste, and that's a shame because it can devalue the athleticism and beauty of the sport.

I cringe every time I see a garish, poorly constructed, or crudely designed costume. Yet bad costumes are almost inevitable. When young skaters begin to perform it is usually their mothers—or someone else's mother, or a lady at the club—who lovingly designs and sews their costumes. As the skaters climb the competitive ladder, most families wouldn't consider using professional designers because of the expense, so a homemade quality of design and workmanship becomes acceptable. Advancing further, a skater's look becomes increasingly important to his or her career, yet parents and coaches retain control over costumes, even though most are no more equipped to design than a designer is to coach.

For half a dozen years I've worked at NBC with Dick Enberg, Tom Hammond, and Greg Gumbel, who are traditional sports anchors. Their questions have helped me to look at skating from the public's perspective. While I was doing color commentary with Greg during the 1995 European Championships, the Ukrainian skater Viacheslav Zagorodniuk stepped on the ice wearing an ornate costume complete with an elaborately beaded headband. On air, a bemused Greg asked the question that was on everyone's mind: "Sandra, what's with the tiara?"

Cultural differences are part of what makes skating colorful and interesting. However, what is accepted in the Ukraine as theatrical may be interpreted as comical or effeminate by a North American audience. Many Russians take their inspiration from the opulent Bolshoi Ballet; their U.S. counterparts would be more likely to draw on the Las Vegas glitter of traditional ice shows.

The look of figure skating has often been controversial. At the 1988 European Championships, Katarina Witt wore an outfit that was cut high on her hips, outraging skating officials as well as some of her competitors, who considered it too risqué. So as not to take any chances, she added

more feathers when she competed at the Calgary Olympics a month later. To me, all the commotion was ridiculous. Kat's dress was certainly overdone, but it was no more revealing than the next skater's. It was her figure, as well as her attitude, that was provocative. Is it any surprise that Kat was almost single-handedly responsible for husbands suddenly sitting down with their wives to watch figure skating?

Even seemingly innocent changes to what is worn on the ice can have unforeseen results. For years I'd noticed that many skaters at competitions looked nowhere near as good as they did in practice, where their simple attire did not upstage their work. Brian Boitano wore running tights during his daily training. As well as being more comfortable, tights were flattering because you could see his incredible leg muscles working. In 1989, we decided that he should have this silhouette in performance as well, and the trend caught on. By 1994, the ISU had banned tights for men from competition on the grounds that they were too balletic for the sport. With rules dictating that women must wear skirts, men must wear sleeves, and cutouts must be filled with flesh-colored fabric, the ISU is trying to control bad taste. If only that were possible!

Rules are only part of the reason costuming can be the most exasperating part of putting the package together. I believe that it is vital to work with professional guidance, so choosing a designer becomes the next challenge. There are very few who specialize in figure skating, and finding the right designer for a specific skater can take years. A designer has to understand that, just like movement and music, the look should be appropriate. Some programs call for ornate costumes; others demand simplicity. Costumes should define the skater's character, reinforce the program's concept, flatter the body, and enhance the movement, but there's a problem if the audience and judges are watching the costume more than the skating.

The construction of a costume is as critical as the design. There are only a few costume builders in North America whose work is superb, so top competitors travel far and wide to have their favorite person make their garments. The way the fabric is cut affects the fit, which is crucial because an uncomfortable costume can upset a performance. If you feel as though something is about to fall off or ride up, you'll be worrying about that instead of concentrating on your skating.

Almost everyone has a costume disaster story. Once, in performance, my brother's nylon zipper on the front of his one-piece jumpsuit split open while we were doing a death spiral. In desperation he fiddled with it with his free hand and somehow got it back together by the time we had completed the move. In the pair and dance events, fabrics can't be too slippery for lifting, or too delicate because they'll rip from all the handling. The crystal in beading can slice a partner's face or get caught so the skaters become attached to each other.

Despite the importance of function, though, it's still the look itself that attracts the most attention from fans and the media, and can influence a skater's career. Coach and choreographer Mary Scotvold wisely asked her friend, couture designer Vera Wang, a former skater herself, to create Nancy Kerrigan's costumes for the 1993 and 1994 seasons. As well as bringing a fashionable look to the ice, those elegant, memorable dresses

"IS IT ANY SURPRISE THAT KAT WAS ALMOST SINGLE-HANDEDLY RESPONSIBLE FOR HUSBANDS SUDDENLY SITTING DOWN WITH THEIR WIVES TO WATCH FIGURE SKATING?"

Kristi Yamaguchi wears hand-painted silk as
Shakespeare's Juliet (facing page); silver lamé
skating to Crystal Water's 100% Pure Love (left);
and an Ozbek-inspired outfit for the Queen ballad
Who Wants to Live Forever (center), all designed by
Frances Dafoe. And a blond wig for a change (right),
with a costume designed by Deborah Ferguson.

played a major role in forming Nancy's serene, sophisticated image.

The best way to consistently guarantee good costumes is to work closely with a designer you trust and provide him or her with detailed direction. One of skating's foremost designers, Jef Billings, has worked for years in film, theater, and television, as well as on skating events such as *Stars on Ice*. He was responsible for creating a variety of looks for Peggy Fleming and Dorothy Hamill, as well as some of Scott Hamilton's most memorable costumes, including one with battery-powered chaser lights running up and down his legs like tuxedo stripes. Jef welcomes a dialogue, and when he brings his ideas forward they are always strong. Before he begins a design, he will listen to a skater's music and, if possible, watch the choreography.

I knew we were taking a risk with Kristi Yamaguchi's "Doop Doop" program because it was offbeat and unexpected. As I'm choreographing, I usually begin to get a notion of how the skater should look, but this time I didn't. All I knew was that the costume could make or break the number, so I said to Jef, "It's up to you to put a smile on everyone's face the moment Kristi steps on the ice." His solution, a whimsical magenta, black, and red outfit that he described as "neo-ragtime," did just that.

The potential for design on the ice is limitless, and there's room for every possible style, from delicate chiffon to denim, from minimalism to extravagance. So long as it's executed with taste and integrity, any costume can work and the impact can be profound. Just as you hear the music when you think of so many great performances, it's often a skater's look that stays in your imagination long after their skates have left the ice.

FACING PAGE | *Skating to Colin James's blues-rock ballad* Why'd You Lie, *Paul Martini (holding his partner, Barb Underhill, aloft) proves the adage "less is more."*

RIGHT | *During his three-minute "Hair" program, Scott Hamilton depicts a baby-boomer life cycle from hippie to yuppie. Beginning with a long-haired wig, headband, and Salvation Army threads, his costume, designed by Jef Billings, evolves into a conservative pin-striped vest and trousers, with plain white shirt and tie. (And, as nature would have it, a receding hairline.)*

ABOVE | *For Maia Usova and
Alexander Zhulin, soft, flowing
silks and muted colors, sensuous
choreography, and romantic music
work together in perfect harmony.*

FACING PAGE | *Olympic and
World Champions Marina Klimova
and Sergei Ponomarenko are known
for their dramatic romanticism,
even using Marina's flowing, exotic
auburn hair to their advantage.*

FACING PAGE | *Philippe Candeloro, the 1994 Olympic bronze medalist from France, leaps at any opportunity to bare his soul.*

LEFT | *Skating to Richard Rodgers's Carousel Waltz in a professional competition, Brian Boitano wears the kind of tights that were eventually banned from ISU competition.*

RIGHT | *Skater as rock star: Kurt Browning in exhibition, performing to Terence Trent D'Arby's Dance Little Sister.*

Stars On Ice

Stars On Ice

ABOVE | Jef's inspiration for Paul's costume was the phrase "never again." Selecting textured fabrics, such as tweeds, and aging them, he also had the words embroidered into the material. "It was the first time I'd had the story written into the costume," Jef said.

Having decided to pair the solos back-to-back at the end of Act One, I knew the lighting had to be perfect. We lit Paul in stark white lights, which brought out the somber grayness of his costume, and complemented his theme. For Kat, we used muted colors to bathe her red dress in a warm light, representing hope and life.

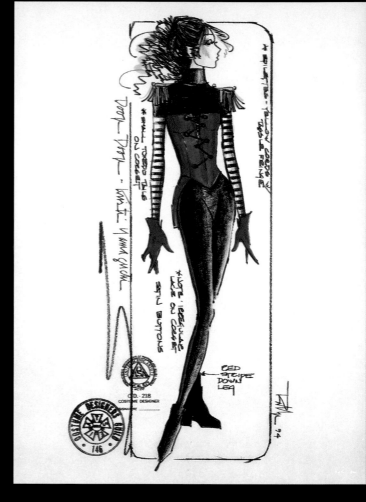

ABOVE | Designer Jef Billings's mission was to put a smile on everyone's face for Kristi Yamaguchi's Doop Doop. His solution: to create a larger-than-life, almost cartoonish costume. Jef thought Kristi's music sounded like a contemporary version of a marching ragtime band, so he chose traditional shapes and decorations—epaulets, stripes, buttons, gloves—and gave them a whimsical twist by making the epaulets oversized and the buttons crooked, and by using bright colors. For a modern touch, he added a corset.

FACING PAGE | Alexei Urmanov, the 1994 Olympic Champion, is well known for his flamboyant costumes, yet his style of skating is clean and precise. Europeans loved this dramatic outfit for his "Swan Lake" program, but it left many North Americans bewildered.

ABOVE | *Standing with Brian Orser and Katarina Witt on location filming* Carmen on Ice, *an unlikely group of matadors— trying their very hardest to look the part—are wearing authentic hand-embroidered costumes. There were even patches covering holes where bulls had gored the real matadors.*

RIGHT | *If Kat was born to play Carmen, the role of Escamillo could only have been* Brian Orser's. *Sitting between takes, he is handsome and comfortable in costume.*

FACING PAGE | *Brian Orser, standing outside the Maestranza bull ring, watches real matadors line up for their photo shoot.*

FOLLOWING PAGES | *Natalia Mishkuteniok's and Artur Dmitriev's costumes balance the masculine and feminine aspects of love, as they skate to Liszt's* Liebestraum.

THE SHOW

*N*ever before have figure skaters had so many opportunities to pursue a professional career. Year-round pro competitions have increased skaters' profiles and earning power, but it is in performance, under the spotlights, night after night, where skaters truly learn to communicate with audiences. As the public's fascination with skating continues to grow, more and more live shows of all sizes are being created around North America, of which *Stars on Ice* and Tom Collins's *World Tour of Figure Skating Champions* are the most prestigious.

This was not always so. Barely a decade ago most leading skaters, once their amateur competitive life ended, disappeared into oblivion. Once they were out of the Olympic stream the media and public lost interest in skaters, whose previous accomplishments were soon forgotten. A few lucky ones became headliners with *Ice Capades* or *Ice Follies* (which became *Walt Disney's World on Ice* in 1981), shows that in their heyday were grand and exciting theatrical extravaganzas, like Ziegfeld Follies transplanted onto a rink.

My involvement in the shows dates back to the early eighties, when I choreographed the principal skaters in *Ice Capades* for several seasons. Eventually I started thinking about how to modernize live skating shows, and how to better integrate the talents of Olympic athletes when they turn professional. Katarina Witt and Brian Boitano gave me that opportunity, inviting me to direct and choreograph their three North American tours beginning in 1990.

Meanwhile, in 1986, *Ice Capades* failed to renew Scott Hamilton's contract. But Scott, a four-time National Champion, four-time World Champion, and Olympic gold medalist, refused to accept the limitations being imposed on his career. He sat down with his agent, Bob Kain at IMG, the world's largest sports management agency, and together they decided to produce a modern show featuring Olympic-caliber skating. They named it *Stars on Ice*, and over the years it has grown into a major tour reaching seventy North American cities, large and small. In 1992, *Stars on Ice* hired me as its director and co-producer.

Our work on the show follows an annual cycle. As soon as the tour ends in May, it's time to plan the next season. Our producer, Byron Allen, and I arrange a brainstorming session with as many of the fourteen-member

cast and eight-member creative team as we can assemble. We discuss the strengths and weaknesses of last year's show and the ways in which we can improve it. We also establish what each skater would like to do next—both individually and as a group. In the summer of 1994, for example, Paul Wylie suggested a production number based on Stomp, the British troupe that uses everyday objects like garbage pails, newspapers, and brooms in its unique blend of percussion and dance. Taking the idea one step further, I asked, "Why use someone else's sound effects when we could use our own?" This led to a piece called "Five Minutes for Icing," which became an ensemble number using a composition by our musical director, Marvin Dolgay, and an associate, Kevan Staples, that incorporated recorded skating sounds and percussion instruments. Next I suggested a "skate-off" between Paul, Scott Hamilton, and Kurt Browning. By strapping microphones near their ankles, we could use the live sound of their skate blades to create their own percussion solos.

Throughout the summer, Michael Seibert, our associate director and choreographer, makes trips back and forth from New York to my home in Toronto. Intellectually curious and intensely creative, Michael is a former Olympic ice dancer with whom I have developed a working relationship that is as exciting as it is productive, which is a good thing since we spend endless hours together on and off the ice. To begin a new production, we listen to hundreds of compact discs and gradually piece together the best ideas. Taking into consideration all of the suggestions made by the skaters and our production team, we also evaluate current trends in fashion and music, as well as the show's mix of talent and personalities. Public reaction is also taken into account. Even though our audience is knowledgeable, it is a broad cross-section of ages and tastes, so we have to make sure there's something for everyone. All of this determines the overall artistic direction we take.

ABOVE | *One of the most charismatic performers, Kurt Browning is a chameleon: he can adapt to any style. On the 1995* Stars on Ice *tour, he's a 1940s "cool cat" moving to the big band sound of Royal Crown Revue's* Hey Pachuco.

As ideas begin to take shape, the collaborative process becomes even more intense. Returning to New York, Michael continues to develop the ideas while Marvin and his partner, Glenn Morley, begin composing and editing the music. I communicate by phone and fax with them as well as our costume designer, Jef Billings, in Los Angeles and our lighting designer, Ken Billington, in New York, who brings his vast experience on Broadway to our show. In the meantime, skaters are working on their individual programs, some at home with their own choreographers, while others are arriving one by one to work with me. It's a giant jigsaw puzzle, and out of all this collaboration a show slowly emerges.

For the 1995-96 season, Scott wanted to do a solo based on the soundtrack of the western movie *Desperado.* That prompted me to think about building a twenty-minute production spoofing a "spaghetti western," with Scott and Katarina Witt, who was with us for the U.S. tour, as featured soloists. We mixed music from *Desperado, Don Juan DeMarco,* and Sergio Leone's *Once Upon a Time in the West.* To this, Marvin added sound effects of horses' hooves, whinnying, and a rattlesnake. Ken ordered "gobos," cutout patterns placed over the light fixtures that, when focused on the ice, created the shape of cactus plants as well as horses' hooves that "walked" across the rink. Jef designed western costumes in earth tones to reinforce the setting of a

RIGHT | *For several weeks we spend hour upon hour rehearsing together on the ice. It can be tedious, frustrating, and cold, but it is also inspiring, rewarding, and fun, and it's always exciting to see the show come to life.*

rough-and-tumble Mexican border town. To complete our comical location, we ordered up a tacky wooden town gate on which hung a pair of fuzzy blue skates.

By the early fall we're ready to begin rehearsals. Byron chooses a facility with two ice surfaces in a city that is most convenient for the majority of our cast and crew, then for three weeks Michael and I, along with our performance director Lea Ann Miller, are on the ice choreographing with the skaters daily from 10 A.M. to 6 P.M. The schedule is demanding. Skaters must learn the show while still finding time to train for competitions. Often they must interrupt rehearsals or give up their days off to fly to competitive events or to honor promotional commitments. Long days on the ice are exhausting, and everyone's feet ache from wearing their skates for so many consecutive hours. Our physiotherapist is on call twenty-four hours a day to work on sore muscles and keep minor injuries from escalating. At the same time, Marvin and Glenn are back in Toronto working on the music and sound effects, while props are being prepared in New York. Backstage, Jef is working with his team readying fifty to sixty costumes for fittings, and the production office is humming with activity.

For the cast, spending so many hours together means that we get to know one another all too well.

Scott, the founder, is the patriarch. A moody, creative, quick-witted man, he is also the quintessential entertainer whose constant joking masks the fact that he cares deeply about the welfare of the cast and the company.

Rosalynn Sumners, known as Roz, has never missed a show in ten years. She's cheerful, animated, and always, always talking.

Kristi's mainly serene personality is leavened by a spirited streak. An astonishingly quick study, she quietly learns her own choreography—and everyone else's, as we once learned in rehearsal when she perfectly performed each and every step and movement of one of Scott's four-minute programs.

Paul, who is intense, passionate, and cerebral, is always, always thinking.

Kat is a force of nature. She trusts her instincts, and is unabashedly forthright. Her boisterous laugh and bawdy sense of humor keep us all amused while she screws up her steps. When she's finally convinced that she's doing it wrong, she'll laugh and say, "Don't worry. I'll learn it, I'll learn it."

Kurt lives life to the fullest. Emotional and unpredictable, he skates hard and plays hard. In rehearsals he used to scare me by impulsively throwing himself into wild jumps, until I made him promise to think before he leaps.

Doug Ladret, the teacher's pet, offers to try out any and all ideas. His partner, the sweet Christine "Tuffy" Hough, is eager to please. Although Olympians, these former Canadian Champions truly came into their own as professionals. Their reputation as hip, sexy skaters performing to funky artists such as Prince and Lenny Kravitz has earned them a cult following.

Elena Bechke and Denis Petrov, who are from St. Petersburg, worked through their divorce one summer between seasons and continued performing happily together. They're the perfectionists, always the first ones on the ice and the last ones off.

ABOVE | *Every time Isabelle Brasseur and Lloyd Eisler perform, they receive a standing ovation for their exceptional and difficult tricks.*
FACING PAGE | *The 1984 Olympic gold medalist and four-time World Champion Scott Hamilton goes head-over-heels for his audience.*

TOP | *Kristi Yamaguchi, as one of the guys, flanked by her "nasty boys," Paul Wylie (left) and Scott Hamilton (right).*

BOTTOM | *To commemorate the tenth anniversary of the Sarajevo Olympics in 1994, we created a tribute to the war-torn region. The skaters, each a medalist at Sarajevo, dressed in the five colors of the Olympic rings. Skating to Elton John's* Funeral for a Friend:

[from left] Brian Orser (men's silver medalist); Kitty Carruthers (pair silver medalist); Scott Hamilton (men's gold medalist); Peter Carruthers (pair silver medalist); and Rosalynn Sumners (women's silver medalist).

For the 1993-94 season, we opened with a Bam. The pop-jazz tune by Candy Dulfer featured Kitty Carruthers (top) getting flipped, Christine Hough (left) getting bounced, and Kristi Yamaguchi (overleaf) getting tossed.

When Ekaterina Gordeeva and Sergei Grinkov were with us, they brought a sense of family to *Stars on Ice*. They had each other, their baby daughter, Daria, and their passion to skate. Sergei, who never learned to speak English, but understood everything that was said, observed us with his twinkling eyes and Cheshire cat smile. Katia, radiant and warmhearted, loved to cook for Sergei and would sometimes bake her special tiramisu for the entire cast. So many other skaters have been a part of *Stars on Ice* over the years, each leaving their individual imprint upon our collective unconscious.

About ten days before we're scheduled to open, our crew, led by production manager Dave Hoffis, arrives to set up our computer-automated lighting rig and our 20,000-watt sound system. We begin lighting the skaters' solos, as well as the production numbers one by one, entering all of the information into a state-of-the-art computerized console. The five-member lighting design team works every day, starting at 8 A.M. and often not finishing until well after midnight. We've spent as long as ten hours lighting a complicated three-minute number. Ken, with board programmer Brad Malkus, a world-renowned system designer, can give me almost anything I want. For Kristi's "Seasons" solo, I requested "a Monet painting," and got an impressionistic wash of colors that slowly painted the ice in rhythm to the music.

After four dress and technical rehearsals, we're as ready as we'll ever be for the inevitably nerve-wracking experience of opening night.

The production numbers are unique because nowhere else can audiences enjoy many of their favorite skating stars working together on the ice. They're also fun for the skaters because it's a rare opportunity for them to interact in performance. For the spaghetti western, we toyed with the skaters' images, knowing audiences would enjoy the inside jokes. We decided Kat should play a mysterious stranger disguised as a man. We cast Kurt Browning as a dusty cowboy who finds himself strangely attracted to this mysterious guy and can't figure out why. Meanwhile, Roz, who's playing the seductive town flirt, makes an unsuccessful play for Kat—probably the first time Roz has ever been rejected, on or off the ice. Scott, who plays straight man to everyone, tries to provoke a fight with Kat, who responds by kissing him.

When scheduling conflicts meant that we lost Kat and Roz for the Canadian portion of the tour, we had to figure out how to replace these irreplaceable women. At Jef's suggestion, we cast six-foot-tall Lloyd Eisler as a man disguised as one ugly woman, which was certainly as absurd a premise as dressing Kat as a man. A good sport, Lloyd took his role seriously. To Bryan Adams's song *Have You Ever Really Loved a Woman?* he amorously chased a horrified Scott. In rehearsals, as we created the choreography, the entire company was doubled over with laughter.

"IT'S A GIANT JIGSAW PUZZLE, AND OUT OF ALL THIS COLLABORATION A SHOW SLOWLY EMERGES."

ABOVE AND RIGHT | *"Sometimes
a guy just has to feel pretty," said
Scott Hamilton the first time he
saw his dancing partner, Lloyd
Eisler, in costume.*

But you never know how an audience will react, so it was with a great sense of satisfaction that we watched as audiences roared with laughter, giving Lloyd standing ovations in every city.

On the road, *Stars on Ice* is like a touring rock band performing one-night stands in cities across North America. Every evening, after the performance, our twelve-member crew spends three hours packing up 80,000 pounds of sound and lighting gear, as well as the props, costumes, and even the skaters' skates. Then two tractor-trailers carrying our gear, and the crew in their bus—equipped with beds—drive to the next city in time for an early morning load-in, at which time they'll begin the four- to five-hour set-up of our rig. The rest of the day is spent readying the building for the skaters' arrival—focusing lights, running sound checks, pressing costumes, and ensuring the ice is at the ideal temperature of twenty-four degrees Fahrenheit.

The lighting director, who calls the show every night, is like a field commander. He has a notebook that looks like a medium-sized city's telephone directory containing hundreds of cues. Finding a good lighting director who has a feel for skating as well as theater is difficult, and over the past seven years I've been lucky enough to have worked with three of the best—David Finley, Jeff Markowitz, and Gregg Maltby. The lighting director's instructions to the board and spot operators, and to the sound man, are as critical as the performance of the skaters, because his timing and artistry set the pace of the show.

Meanwhile, the skaters stay in a hotel overnight in the city where they have just performed, so they've had a chance to rest before flying to the next stop. We also have a custom-built bus for the cast that takes them to and from airports, hotels, and arenas, and occasionally from one city to the next if the distance isn't too great. Still, the endless routine of travel, anonymous hotel rooms, catered meals, and isolation from home and family is tiring.

Eventually, the cast settles into the groove of life on the road, although for many, adjusting to this life may take years. As young skaters preparing for the Olympics, the world revolves around you and your training only. As a professional, you have a responsibility to perform and to please audiences nightly, as well as to attend press conferences, meet with sponsors, and sign autographs. Add to this keeping up a rigorous training program

while living out of a suitcase. I've heard skaters say that life as a professional is even more difficult than training for the Olympics.

For those who love performing, however, the satisfaction can be enormous. Standing at center ice during *Stars on Ice* shows, Scott Hamilton often tells his audiences, "I am the happiest, the most *myself,* when I'm here on the ice, skating for you."

LEFT | *Shooting Chrysler Stars on Ice in Toronto for CBC-TV. On my left, stage manager Don McNeill. On my right, John Brunton, a veteran producer of documentaries, specials, and TV series, who has a passion for putting figure skating on the screen.*

ABOVE | *In* Stars on Ice, *Kristi has been able to explore her interest in the classics. With Natalia Annenko and Genrikh Sretenski (left) as the Capulets and Elena Bechke and Denis Petrov (right) as the Montagues, Kristi portrays Shakespeare's Juliet. At the end of the number, a narrator's voice reads: "Death, that hath suck'd the honey of thy breath/Hath had no power yet upon thy beauty."*

LEFT | *Kristi, standing in a pool of cherry blossoms, in a solo based on Puccini's* Madama Butterfly.

FACING PAGE | *I wouldn't normally allow a skater to do an improvisation because it's so difficult as well as risky. When Gary Beacom asked to do an improv using Led Zeppelin's* You Shook Me, *however, I said: "Let's give it a shot." Like all improvs, some nights were better than others but it was always fascinating to watch Gary think on his skates.*

ABOVE | *Every day, before the show, the skaters warm up on the ice for forty-five minutes. From left: Christine Hough and Doug Ladret; Natalia Annenko and Genrikh Sretenski; and Ekaterina Gordeeva and Sergei Grinkov.*

FACING PAGE | *For our 1995–96 opening number, the cast wore beautiful ivory costumes. Michael Seibert had the marvelous idea of spray-painting Kurt Browning with graffiti as a transition into his solo number which followed. Our costume designer, Jef Billings, had to figure out how to do this without adding thousands of dollars to our costume budget. After much experimentation, he discovered spray paint and fabrics that were completely washable.*

For celebrity skaters like Scott Hamilton and Katarina Witt, signing autographs is part of life on the road. "I like meeting the public directly," says Kat.

accessible to, and appreciative of, his audience. When he founded Stars on Ice ten years ago, it was based on a simple love of skating, and that premise hasn't changed. Today,

ABOVE | Life on the road means planes and buses, airports, hotel rooms, and bad catering. For many, it also means leaving loved ones behind. Doug Ladret (top left) is lucky; his wife, Lara, a physio-therapist, travels with the company. But everyone looks forward to visits. Having flown her parents in from Berlin, Katarina Witt (bottom right) videotapes them at Madison Square Garden in New York. Before the Berlin Wall came down in 1989, they were never allowed to travel as a family.

ABOVE | *As the tour continues,*
you sometimes wake up wondering
which city you're in. But the cama-
raderie of the group, personal contact
with fans, and the performances
make life on the road worthwhile.

FOLLOWING PAGES | *Skating*
with Pride *(by Robert Clivilles and*
David Cole).

127

T H E   S C R E E N

Whenever I see figure skating on film or video, I'm struck by the incredible potential of the electronic media. The camera can capture every possible point of view, from close-ups of a skater's face to wide shots that take in the whole panorama. Although nothing can duplicate the excitement and energy of seeing a live performance, I love the challenge of choreographing for the camera, of capturing the motion, as well as the emotion, of skating on-screen.

My first experience in choreographing skating for the screen came in 1984 when I acted as associate choreographer on Dorothy Hamill's TV special, *Romeo & Juliet on Ice*. The possibilities for figure skating on TV and film fascinated me, although it would be a few years before skating's popularity grew large enough to make those opportunities possible.

Shortly after Brian Boitano won the gold medal at the 1988 Olympics, ABC agreed to create a one-hour special for him, the first time an American male skater had ever been given his own network prime-time show. A group of us, including the producer, Amy Sacks Feld, and producer-director, Doug Wilson, came up with a premise: the ice is a blank canvas with limitless possibilities. Skating outdoors is always a liberating experience, and one of Brian's dreams was to find the ultimate sheet of natural ice. His dream, he said, was "to skate on a glacier in Alaska." Naively, we all said: "Great, let's go."

Off on our adventure to begin shooting what would become *Canvas of Ice*, we flew with a crew to Anchorage, Alaska, where we hired a helicopter pilot as a scout. He found an unnamed glacial lake in the wilderness surrounded by snow-covered mountains. When the pilot dropped me on the ice to see whether it was skateable, I found a surface the size of several football fields that had miraculously frozen as smooth as an Olympic rink. The ten-foot-thick ice was so clear that I could see rocks on the bottom of the lake. Having confirmed with the pilot that we'd found our spot, he flew away to get the others, leaving me alone. Under blue, cloudless skies, I stood in the middle of nowhere, gusts of wind ringing in the immense silence. Lying down on the ice, I felt the powerful heat of the sun

FACING PAGE | *Katarina Witt, playing the title role in the 1990 film* Carmen on Ice. *Arrested by a young soldier, Don Jose (played by Brian Boitano), she seductively dances the seguidilla to convince him to set her free.*

RIGHT | Canvas of Ice: *a dream come true in Alaska. Not only did Brian Boitano have to deal with the natural elements, but our hovering helicopter contributed to the high winds.*

ABOVE | *For Lillas Pastia's bar in* Carmen, *this sixteenth-century Moorish ruin was transformed into a magnificent set combining the real with the surreal.*

LEFT | *Several months before shooting* Carmen, *director Horant H. Hohlfeld and I did a site survey on location outside Seville, Spain.*

despite a temperature of thirty below. Hearing a sound beneath me as loud as a sonic boom, I leapt to my feet in terror, sure that the ice was breaking up. A fifty-foot-long hairline crack had appeared, although the surface was as solid as ever. In the raw glory of nature, figure skating suddenly seemed so insignificant.

Once our pilot had brought Brian, the crew, and our supplies, we set up "camp," which consisted of a pup tent and a gas heater. Despite sunny skies, a freezing wind tore across the lake. A skater with less than Brian's physical strength wouldn't have been able to launch triple jumps into that wind. While the rest of us bundled up in snow suits and heavy parkas, for the camera Brian wore only a thin cotton shirt and several layers of tights. Once we began shooting, we worked in short sequences, then huddled around the heater trying to warm up between takes.

Our crew managed to hide in the landscape giant speakers connected to a sound system that blasted our music as though down from the heavens. The weather stayed clear, and for four perfect days Brian skated take after take while we videotaped wide shots from the side of a hill and aerial shots from the helicopter.

To capture the speed and movement of skating, we used a unique system Doug Wilson had devised over the years, which involved our cameraman, the revered wildlife cinematographer D'Arcy Marsh, cradling his camera while being pushed in a wheelchair. Since I was the only other one on skates and knew the choreography well enough to anticipate Brian's movements, I found myself pushing D'Arcy across the ice with all my strength, swinging around every time Brian made a turn, gasping lungfuls of frigid air. Once in awhile, a wheel would stick in a rut and D'Arcy and I would tumble. By the final day, we were exhausted, but we all knew that our efforts had produced some of the most extraordinary skating footage ever.

To complete the special we went to Toronto, Paris, and East Germany with Katarina Witt. But those few of us who experienced the Alaska shoot treasure the memory of our adventure with Brian as he skated his heart out on the top of the world.

ABOVE | *Discussing movement with Horant. Carmen was his first experience filming figure skating, so it was important for me to have him see it through my eyes.*

As a choreographer for live shows, I'm conscious of working in an arena surrounded by an audience, where the program has to look equally pleasing from all sides. In competitions, the same is true, although I may favor the side where the judges are sitting. Doing *Canvas of Ice*, I learned the importance of choreographing to the camera. Will it be a wide shot, a head-to-toe shot or a close-up? Close-ups provide the detail audiences never see at live performances. Intimately watching a skater's face captures the emotion of a moment. Head-to-toe and wide shots must be carefully planned because a movement can look spectacular from one angle and static from another. The lower the camera is placed, the higher the jump will look. Jumping toward the camera is always more dramatic than jumping away from it, although jumping across the frame is also effective because viewers can see the height and distance.

Live performances are ephemeral; they exist only for the moment. In TV or film, skaters do multiple retakes, both to make the performance as perfect as possible and to allow the cameras to record different perspectives.

Since skating is so physically demanding, learning to work in front of the cameras is a technique unto itself.

I had to apply all of this knowledge under trying circumstances when I worked on Katarina Witt's *Carmen on Ice,* a full-length feature film, in 1989. Ever since using the music from *Carmen* for her long program during the 1988 season, Kat had dreamed of making a film of Georges Bizet's opera about a flirtatious gypsy cigarette girl killed by a jealous lover. The producer, Thomas Bürger, an East German defector, gathered a cast and crew of North Americans, East and West Germans, Spaniards, and Hungarians to shoot the film over four weeks on location near Seville, Spain. The common language, thank goodness, was English. In the lead roles, Brian Boitano played Carmen's ingenuous lover, Don Jose, Brian Orser appeared as Escamillo, a dashing toreador, and Kat's Carmen, of course, was a role she'd been born to play.

Having managed to work with Kat, Brian Boitano, and Brian Orser in Toronto for only two weeks, we choreographed just twelve minutes of the ninety-minute film by the time we started a week of rehearsals in East Berlin. I'll never forget the sobering experience as we crossed through the Berlin Wall at Checkpoint Charlie to reach our hotel and the rink. It was October 1989, and every day we saw peaceful demonstrations in the streets, and sensed a growing tension in the air. Little did we know that in a matter of weeks, the East German government would open its borders to the West and begin tearing down the wall, ending four decades of separation.

By the time we reached our principal location—the beautiful ruins of a Moorish castle about an hour's drive from Seville—the crew had constructed an elaborate set, complete with a portable rink, smaller than normal size, at one hundred feet long and sixty feet wide, that perfectly blended with the ruins. Because so many scenes had to be shot in darkness, we began at four in the afternoon and worked through the night until sunrise, day in and day out. I created most of the choreography on the spot, a minute at a time, while the crew of two hundred people stood around waiting for me to complete a sequence so we could film it. Looking at all these expectant faces, I would sometimes turn away, take a deep breath, and say to myself, "Okay, what am I going to do next?"

As with most films, we were shooting out of sequence. It was my responsibility to make sure the choreography correctly reflected the storyline and character development, even though our schedule barely allowed time to prepare from shot to shot, let alone think about the big picture. Knowing that Kat and Brian were singles skaters unaccustomed to working as a pair, I'd recruited Michael Seibert as my assistant choreographer. With his background as an ice dancer, combined with mine as a pair skater, we would work out each movement together and teach it to them.

What an ordeal for Kat and Brian! After training for years on a full-sized rink, they had to learn to skate on a smaller surface crowded with extras. Under most circumstances, skaters rarely wear their skates for longer than a few hours a day; here, Kat and Brian wore theirs for twelve consecutive hours every night. I've often wondered how their feet could ever have recovered. Although I worried about having to come up with the choreography under pressure, it was Kat and Brian who not only had to learn each sequence but then also

"I LEARNED THE JOY OF COLLABORATING WITH HUNDREDS OF TALENTED PEOPLE TO TAKE AN IDEA ONTO THE ICE, AND FROM THERE ONTO THE SCREEN. THESE SHARED EXPERIENCES CREATE A SPECIAL BOND THAT LASTS A LIFETIME."

TOP AND BOTTOM | *According to the script, Carmen "forces Don Jose to move to the rhythm and starts to play with him like a puppy on a leash." Working with the rope was especially difficult because Kat and Brian kept getting tangled up, resulting in many hilarious outtakes.*

ABOVE | At the end of the seguidilla, when a smitten
Don Jose loosens the rope to allow her to escape,
Carmen knocks him to the ground and runs away,
with the crowd in pursuit. A German actor (left,
under archway) was hired to play the role of Zuniga,
the sergeant who ordered Carmen's arrest. Like most
actors, he exaggerated on his resumé, claiming he
could skate. For his one skating scene, we had to push
him into frame with exactly the right force so that
he would glide to a stop a foot away from Katarina.

TOP LEFT | *Choreographing the habanera. It's fun working with Kat because we're the same height and have similar figures, so it's like working with a mirror image of myself. We relate to each other like sisters.*

BOTTOM LEFT | *Midway through filming Carmen, the Berlin Wall came down. Kat's reaction was a mixture of jubilation, confusion, and anxiety. The East German system had generously supported*

her and given her special privileges, yet it had also constantly frustrated her efforts to work outside the country and taken most of her earnings. Having experienced political freedom through her travels in the West, she was excited for her country. But it also meant the end of a system that had provided her security and her identity. For the campfire scene filmed that night, Carmen had just

read of her approaching death in her tea leaves. Contributing to Kat's pensive expression as she stared into the flames were thoughts about the death of her former life as one of Communist East Germany's elite athletes.

RIGHT | *Once, at 4 A.M., with the ice rough and pock-marked with holes, Kat had to land a triple toe-loop on our unusually small ice surface. After more than thirty takes Kat was exhausted*

and desperate. Anyone else would have quit, but not Kat. "I'm gonna land this damn jump if it takes me a hundred times," she said. Willing to try anything, she approached my husband, Dino, rubbed the top of his bald head for good luck, and landed the jump. From then on, Dino's bald spot was Kat's good luck charm.

had to perform it, take after take. As everyone grew increasingly exhausted, and some fell sick, we devised strategies to get us through the night. Kat's energy often collapsed around 5 A.M., when she would become giddy and laugh helplessly. Someone would slip her a chocolate and she would recover enough to film a few more takes before exhaustion would overcome her again.

The biggest threats to an outdoor ice surface are direct sunlight and rain, both of which cause ice to melt. Midway through the shoot, with two critical scenes left, it began raining steadily. It rained in Spain harder than it had in over a century. Finally, after ten wasted days, we gave up, and a month later relocated to our practice rink in Berlin. Returning to visit the new friends we'd made during rehearsals, we found a bittersweet jubilation. The long oppression finally gone, they were happy and celebrating, but uncertain about their future. A few of them had found work with our crew, recreating the set so authentically that even we could barely tell the difference, and we completed the film in only ten days. After *Carmen on Ice* ran on the U.S. cable-TV network HBO, Kat and the two Brians won prestigious Emmy Awards for outstanding achievement in classical music/dance programming.

The making of *Carmen* was often grueling, but I learned the joy of collaborating with hundreds of talented people to take an idea onto the ice, and from there onto the screen. These shared experiences create a special bond that lasts a lifetime. Usually a production starts with a handful of people throwing ideas around a room, which can be a stimulating and inspiring exercise setting the stage for exceptional work. Making Kurt Browning's 1994 TV special, *You Must Remember This,* was one of these magical experiences. I had worked with the producer, John Brunton, and the director, Joan Tosoni, a couple of years earlier when we'd made Kurt's first special, *Tall in the Saddle*. For that one, our intention had been to introduce Kurt to the TV audience. To show his roots, we shot it on location in and around his hometown of Caroline, Alberta, and included his parents and friends. By 1994, though, he had grown up and moved to Toronto. By now a four-time World Champion, he had also experienced back trouble and a disappointing Olympics, so he knew both triumph and hardship. Since the Canadian public knew him and adored him, and he had developed impressively over the years, we decided to address the question: What is Kurt's range as a performer on the ice?

To highlight his comic talents, Kurt portrayed a clown for an audience of children. To emphasize his rock-star image, we shot a music-video-on-skates to Robert Palmer's hit song *Simply Irresistible,* in which a flirtatious Kurt cavorted with three beautiful women—Kristi Yamaguchi, Christine Hough, and three-time Canadian Champion Josée Chouinard. And to reveal the influence of his ballet training, we created a classical scene with the Canadian National Ballet's Tomas Schramek.

LEFT | *The pipes beneath our portable ice surface. Our multinational crew of Germans, Hungarians, and Spaniards, who knew nothing about figure skating, didn't understand that walking across the ice wearing street shoes left debris that could damage the edge of a skate blade and send a skater into a bad fall. Also, we'd painted the ice a yellowish earth tone and every time we'd turn our backs the crew would helpfully repaint it and scatter straw to add to the atmosphere. We had to explain to them that you can't skate over straw or fresh paint.*

TOP LEFT | *Kat, Brian, and me in consultation, between takes, wrapped in blankets to protect us from the damp and cold.*

BOTTOM LEFT | *Skating a cameo role for kicks, I danced a farandola with Sean McGill, a gifted Canadian skater who later died of complications arising from AIDS.*

RIGHT | *A dream sequence featuring Kat and Brian Orser, who played the role of matador Escamillo, her new lover.*

TOP | *Ekaterina Gordeeva and Sergei Grinkov in Disney's* Greatest Hits on Ice.

CENTER | *Elizabeth Manley's CBC special,* Back to the Beanstalk.

BOTTOM | *The casino scene from "The Big Melt" in Kurt Browning's CBC special,* You Must Remember This.

FACING PAGE | *In Disney's* Greatest Hits on Ice, *Katarina Witt (center) plays Cinderella's wicked stepmother with Marina Klimova (left) and Nancy Kerrigan (right) as her two ugly daughters.*

Our most important goal, though, was to showcase Kurt's acting, his sense of timing, and ability to portray a character. Two sequences became the centerpieces of the show. One, "The Big Melt," spoofed a Humphrey Bogart-style 1940s detective movie. Filmed in black and white, Kurt portrayed a laconic, hard-boiled detective involved with three femme fatales played by Kristi, Christine, and Josée. But the most impressive and technically challenging number was recreating the famous title song number from the Gene Kelly movie *Singin' in the Rain*.

We had all been inspired by Gene Kelly. Kurt used to dream about being Gene Kelly and I used to dream about dancing with Gene Kelly. John Brunton had always wanted to produce a movie like *Singin' in the Rain*, and Joan Tosoni had always wanted to direct a movie like it. We knew we had to do justice to this celebrated scene or not try the number at all.

Our CBC crew spent three months building the set, and three days setting it up in an arena north of Toronto. Our production designer, Russell Chick, was responsible for recreating an authentic-looking 1920s street that ran the full length of the two-hundred-foot-long arena, complete with old-fashioned storefronts and working streetlamps frozen into the ice. The ice surface itself had been meticulously painted to look like asphalt streets and concrete sidewalks. Our special effects team draped 2,300 feet of firehose along the top of the set, and pumped 700 gallons of water through it to create a downpour under which Kurt skated the number. Our director of photography, Maris Jansons, had to pay special attention to lighting the scene because it's so difficult to capture the appearance of natural rainfall on film. Trying to prevent the ice from melting was a constant problem. We could only shoot thirty seconds at a time before everyone available had to take oversized squeegees to push away the pools of water.

Despite the hardships and the technical challenges of the number, the morale was always high. Kurt, whose costume was perpetually drenched, and who constantly struggled to skate through the weight of pouring water, was in heaven and would have performed forever.

In the end, we spent ten hours filming this four-minute number, but it's been described as the best skating scene ever created on screen. Kurt so lived up to his screen idol that it was as though the spirit of Gene Kelly himself had laced up skates that day.

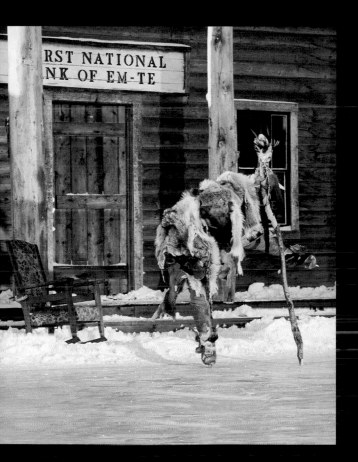

Kurt Browning's 1992 CBC special, Tall in
the Saddle, shot in and around his hometown of
Caroline, Alberta.

LEFT | *Gary Beacom playing the devil in a
scene shot in Em-te town, a reproduction of a
nineteenth-century western town located
outside Caroline.*

TOP RIGHT | *Kurt looks right at home playing
the part of the cowboy.*

BOTTOM RIGHT | *Kurt on horseback: a scene
reflecting his roots. His father, Dewey Browning,
a retired hunting guide, came from a long line
of cowboys.*

ABOVE | *Motivation for moovement. Elizabeth Manley playing Jack Junior in her special,* Back to the Beanstalk. *I reached the pinnacle of my career choreographing a cow*

RIGHT | *Little did I know that I would eventually be a cow, in Kurt Browning's* Tall in the Saddle. *At least I was able to choose the front end.*

LEFT | *Brian Orser has had several award-winning CBC specials, including this one,* Blame It on the Blues. *Brian had always wanted to work with animation, and when a show came along that gave him that chance, I assisted by skating the role of the crocodile, Blue. Later, drawing inspiration from my movements, the animator created Blue frame by frame.*

TOP RIGHT | *For Disney's* Christmas on Ice, *taped in Squaw Valley, California, we used a variation on the wheelchair camera technique used for* Canvas of Ice. *This time I wore a helmet equipped with a cordless antenna that sent the camera feed to a monitor so the director could watch the shot.*

BOTTOM RIGHT | *In* Night Moves, *another of Brian Orser's CBC specials, he is joined by a capella pop group The Nylons singing* Call My Name. *We created a sidewalk for The Nylons using a plastic material called Slick, which you can skate on. This allowed Brian to "magically" jump from the ice surface onto the sidewalk and back again.*

TOP | *For Kurt Browning's CBC special* You Must Remember This, *we used a "drop" for a rock-video sequence skated to Robert Palmer's* Simply Irresistible.

RIGHT | *We flooded the ice with water to get Kurt's reflection in this shot.*

FAR RIGHT | *Shooting on film is far more difficult and time-consuming than shooting on videotape. Director of photography Maris Jansons (far left) had to learn to keep focus while Kurt covered a great distance at high speed.*

ABOVE | *Watching the playback monitor (from left) Christine Hough; Kurt Browning (kneeling); Josée Chouinard; me; cameraman Andy Binnington; dance choreographer Clarence Ford; director Joan Tosoni; and producer John Brunton.*

FOLLOWING PAGES | TOP LEFT | *Final scene from "The Big Melt." Kurt Browning as Bogie and Christine Hough as Breathless, with Michael Slipchuk (lying on the ice), playing a gangster.*

BOTTOM LEFT | *The "Singin' in the Rain" set, with jets of water in view.*

FACING PAGE | *Kurt Browning in "Singin' in the Rain."*

FOLLOWING SPREAD | *The spectacular casino scene, from Kurt Browning's* You Must Remember This.

CHAPTER 9

THE FAMILY

*A*ll top figure skaters and the people who surround them are like a large, rambunctious family. At practice sessions, competitions, professional shows, and promotional engagements, we have seen each other at our happiest and saddest, our strongest and most vulnerable. When you choose a creative pursuit and succeed at it, a large part of your life is necessarily solitary, obsessive, and self-centered, which makes your family of peers that much more important. Within the family are people who have shared your experiences and can sympathize with the tremendous sacrifices you have made.

That isn't to say we aren't sometimes a dysfunctional family. We always gossip (often about the first person who leaves the room), and occasionally we feel ill will toward each other. From time to time there is disagreement and dissension, but in the end our common bond proves to be stronger than any cracks in the foundation. As any family should, we accept and respect each other despite being competitors, despite any past rifts, and despite any differences we may have in family backgrounds, or cultural values, or politics, or sexual orientation.

The extended family includes loyal fans whose support is warm and heartfelt. One sweet moment involved Kurt Browning at a Sunlife *Stars on Ice* performance in Toronto in April 1995, in front of 20,000 members of his extended family. We were video-taping the show for television, and at the end of the performance we asked the audience to stay behind while we shot some retakes. Without warning, I handed the microphone to Kurt and asked him to entertain the crowd for a few minutes until the first skater was ready. As he bantered with the audience, a child asked him whether he was married, and Kurt said, "No, but as a matter of fact my girlfriend, Sonia Rodriguez, is here in the audience somewhere." To our collective amazement, he located her, spontaneously dropped to one knee, and proposed marriage.

Along with the support of the family, the importance of skating as a form of self-expression proves invaluable in times of crisis. In my years of

FACING PAGE | The Skating Family: Hartford, Connecticut, February 27, 1996. Ekaterina Gordeeva (center, facing away), holding her daughter Daria.
RIGHT | *Marina Zoueva's son, thirteen-year-old Fedor Andreev, who was born the year Ekaterina Gordeeva and Sergei Grinkov started skating together.*

ABOVE | *Kurt Browning's girlfriend, Sonia, says yes.*

FACING PAGE | *Barbara Underhill and Paul Martini's eulogy to Barbara's daughter Stephanie, at the 1993 World Professional Championships in Landover, Maryland.*

working with Barbara Underhill and Paul Martini, we lived through great moments of pride and accomplishment, as well as humiliating moments of defeat. In 1993, when one of Barbara's eight-month-old twin daughters drowned in the family pool, Barb said that those skating experiences helped her get through this devastation in her life. Almost immediately she decided to get on the ice in order to express her grief. Having chosen Michael Bolton's version of Lennon and McCartney's *Yesterday* for their music, she found solace in training every day with Paul and me. Skating was clearly the most effective form of therapy for Barb. Later that year, when she and Paul performed the program at the World Professional Championships, I was acting as a color commentator for NBC. I don't think I could describe the emotional power of that performance. Six months pregnant with my son, Dean, I sat beside my co-host, broadcaster Tom Hammond, with tears streaming down my face, unable to utter a word.

Against all odds, two years later, I found myself in the middle of another crisis that rocked the entire skating family and, at the same time, proved the healing power of its ties.

I'll never forget the day that Sergei Grinkov died.

It happened on November 20, 1995, in Lake Placid while we were rehearsing for a new season of *Stars on Ice*. Sergei and Katia Gordeeva, his wife and partner, were practicing with their longtime choreographer, Marina Zoueva, when Sergei said he felt dizzy. He lay down on the ice and died almost immediately, a victim, we later learned, of undiagnosed congenital heart disease.

The entire *Stars on Ice* family was in shock. Everyone adored and respected Katia, Sergei, and their three-year-old daughter, Daria. Considered the most beautiful and elegant pair skaters ever, Gordeeva and Grinkov were also good and kind people, as committed to skating as any of their peers. They also had a perfect relationship together, filled with love and tenderness. Everyone was aware of this on a daily basis. We would see them off to one side stealing a kiss or just exchanging affectionate looks. When Dasha, which is Daria's nickname, would arrive she'd make us smile, and Katia and Sergei were devoted parents. They had a grounding effect on the *Stars on Ice* family, a constant reminder that there is life beyond figure skating and a professional touring show. Yes, it is possible to have it all.

At the time of Sergei's death, we were supposed to open our fifty-five-city, tenth-anniversary American tour in five days, but we hadn't even started our technical rehearsals. Despite our emotional turmoil, we decided to stay in Lake Placid to continue rehearsing the show, partly because we had to, but mainly because it kept us together, and helped us begin to work through the tragedy.

Our opening was postponed for a week, and as the day approached we knew the show still wasn't ready. We couldn't do our opening production number in front of an audience because we hadn't even managed to hold a dress rehearsal. Instead, I placed the skaters in a circle in the center of the rink, holding hands. They were wearing white, with black ribbons on their shirts. I thought it would open the show in a way that expressed

"WE HAVE SEEN EACH OTHER AT OUR HAPPIEST AND SADDEST, OUR STRONGEST AND MOST VULNERABLE. . . . WITHIN THE FAMILY ARE PEOPLE WHO HAVE SHARED YOUR EXPERIENCES AND CAN SYMPATHIZE WITH THE TREMENDOUS SACRIFICES YOU HAVE MADE."

our emotional state. We were in mourning, but the circle also symbolized unity, the strength of the family together. I wasn't sure how the audience would react, but the impact was breathtaking. No one applauded; there was just a reverent silence. Scott took the microphone, and with an emotional voice explained that it was going to be a difficult show, that the evening was dedicated to Sergei. At the end of Act One, instead of a minute of silence, we played all five minutes of Sergei and Katia's music, which was Grieg's Piano Concerto in A minor, and lit the empty ice with a single spotlight. That was our eulogy.

Within twenty-four hours of Sergei's death, the *Stars on Ice* management, production team, and skaters had agreed to do something for Katia. That impulse evolved into the idea of a benefit special, with the proceeds going to Katia and Dasha. CBS, which has a strong commitment to figure skating, and where we'd made many close friends over the years, came on board almost immediately. By the new year, we began planning the benefit, basing the date of the show on several considerations. Estimating that by late February Katia might welcome a project to work on, we hoped perhaps she would even make a public appearance. After studying our *Stars on Ice* schedule, we selected the Hartford Civic Center on February 27, the closest stop on the tour to Katia's home in Simsbury, Connecticut.

Katia had stayed in Moscow for several weeks of mourning after the funeral, and during that time she decided that she wanted to do more than make an appearance at the benefit. She wanted to skate; she *had* to skate. I think everyone was shocked to hear that. I couldn't imagine her on the ice, and I certainly couldn't imagine her on the ice without Sergei. But who were we to make that decision? After all, the show was for her.

Later in January, when Marina and Katia were in Ottawa, Michael Seibert and I flew there to see them. I caught my breath at the sight of Katia alone on the ice. She was very excited to see us, and nervous about showing us the program she and Marina had choreographed. As she began to skate their exquisite work to Mahler's Symphony no. 5, IV Adagietto: Sehr Langsam, I understood how right it was for her.

That day we also talked about a finale for the show. Marina and Katia wanted to use Tchaikovsky's Fifth Symphony, and they had a marvelous idea of using the other skaters, frozen like sculptures, to recreate Gordeeva and Grinkov positions from their most famous programs.

Now it was up to Michael and me to create a show. We started with the idea of interspersing throughout the evening video footage of landmark Gordeeva and Grinkov performances and the skaters' memories of Sergei. In addition to the *Stars on Ice* cast—Scott Hamilton, Kristi Yamaguchi, Paul Wylie, Katarina Witt, Kurt Browning, Rosalynn Sumners, and three couples: Elena Bechke and Denis Petrov, Christine Hough and Doug Ladret, and Susanna Rahkamo and Petri Kokko—we could accommodate six or seven special guests. Although every major skater in the world wanted to be included, Katia chose fellow team member Alexander Fadeev, and Olympic dance champions Marina Klimova and Sergei Ponomarenko. She also invited Viktor Petrenko and Oksana Baiul, who were neighbors of Sergei's and Katia's in Simsbury. Her other guests included Yuka Sato, the young

PREVIOUS PAGES |
Opening night: Discover Card Stars on Ice, *December 2, 1995.*
FACING AND FOLLOWING
PAGE | *Ekaterina Gordeeva skating to Mahler's Fifth Symphony, for her tribute to Sergei, choreographed by Marina Zoueva.*

Japanese World Champion, and Brian Boitano, both skaters Sergei had known and admired. Finally, Katia invited Fedor Andreev, Marina's thirteen-year-old son. He was born the year Sergei and Katia started skating together, and they used to babysit him.

Along with the interviews and skating footage, we prepared two montages depicting Sergei and Katia's life together. CBS had previously produced one, and I asked Kathie Farrell, an independent TV producer, and a long-time friend and associate of ours, to produce the other. The music accompanying it was Ella Fitzgerald's version of Gershwin's *The Man I Love*, and Kathie poured her heart into it, perfectly capturing their tender relationship.

We spent about six weeks doing detailed pre-production, discussing costumes with our designer Jef Billings, music with Marvin Dolgay, sending notes to skaters, and having phone conversations with everyone involved. I was in constant communication with Katia, and her wishes drove every decision. *Stars on Ice* was in Orlando a week before the Hartford date, so Michael and I flew there with our lighting designer, Ken Billington. Although the skaters had to move on, we had a day to light our entire three-hour show with our wonderful technical crew, who had agreed to work on their day off. Michael and I also found time to stage the opening production number.

We had all the skaters in Hartford on the day before the show for only three hours to teach them the opening and closing numbers, and have their first and only costume fitting. Trisha Ricci, our production administrator and my stepdaughter, had plotted on a computer the choreography that Michael and I had set in Orlando, so we could point to the diagrams and say to each skater, "This is where you start and where you're going to be moving to." The next afternoon we had our only dress rehearsal.

To the piano chords of Beethoven's *Moonlight Sonata,* used by Sergei and Katia for their 1994 Olympic long program, the lights were to come up on twenty skaters standing in a circle, wearing black and white as Sergei and Katia had. One by one they broke away and took positions around the rink. They then formed a straight line, like a funeral procession, and slowly walked up the ice. For the final move, they gathered together, held each other's waists, and did a long, slow glide.

I knew that the skaters weren't going to be able to learn all the musical cues with so little preparation, so Michael, Ken, Jeff Markowitz, our lighting director, and I devised a plan to direct the skaters with the lighting. We used what are called "special focus" lights. We told everyone that if they didn't know their musical cue all they had to do was watch for their individual "special" and when they saw it, that was their cue to go. It was up to Jeff to learn all the choreography, read the musical score, and cue the lights.

I asked the skaters to watch the videos during the dress rehearsal, because I knew that seeing Sergei and Katia would be difficult for them. I had been going through pictures and videotapes for months, but they'd been touring or competing in skating competitions, so they were all at different emotional stages of coming to terms with his death. I didn't want them to experience their first reactions to the videos during the live show.

The show brought everyone to the same point, brought us all together around Katia. But she led the way with her strength. The epitome of refinement and purity, it was important to everyone involved that we lived up to Katia.

At the end of Act One, pale blue lights gently lit the ice to the opening strains of Mahler's Fifth. As Katia glided onto the ice, the audience spontaneously rose and gave her a prolonged and thundering ovation that seemed to shake the building. Katia was so taken aback that she hesitated and began to cry, but fought back her tears, continuing her performance even though the applause didn't end for another thirty seconds and most of the audience didn't sit down until she was well into her program. In a transcendent five minutes of skating, Katia shared with us her grief, love, hope, and gratitude.

The Sergei Grinkov benefit, *A Celebration of a Life,* was one of the most powerful evenings of my life. The sentiments expressed there, and the selfless dedication on the part of everyone involved, went far beyond a professional figure skating show, beyond figure skating itself. Directing the show from my vantage point behind the lighting board, with Michael at my side, I spent most of the night sobbing, as did most of the audience. We were honoring a member of our family, whose untimely passing reminded us of the important things in our lives.

At the end of the show, Katia addressed the audience: "I don't have enough words but I also want to wish to all of you, try to find happiness in every day and spend your life with lots of smiles, like at least one smile to each other every day. And say just once extra time that you love the person who live with you, you know, just, just say I love you. It's so great. Thanks everyone. Thank you."

FACING PAGE | **LEFT** | *Katia with her daughter Daria.*

RIGHT | *Katia with Sergei's mother, Anna.*

ABOVE | *Finding hope on the ice, Katia skates the finale to Tchaikovsky's Fifth Symphony.*

FOLLOWING PAGES | A Celebration of a Life, February 27, 1996.

THE PASSION

*W*hen my two-year-old son Dean tells me to sit and watch him "skate" around the family room, I wonder what it is about skating that has captured his imagination. Is it the power, the speed, the dancing, the jumping, the music, the applause? Has he already figured out that his skating will win my approval, or is the desire genetically encoded? Or is it just a phase, like his previous passion for pushing the vacuum cleaner? As I watch him joyfully performing, I experience conflicting feelings. Skating has been my life, but do I want it to be his?

If he chooses to skate, and if he grows up to be anything like the people I've had the privilege of working with over the years, then I should be happy. Having recognized their passion, these women and men are dedicated and disciplined, and live with a sense of purpose. They have the courage to set goals and work toward them, then in performance try their very hardest to live up to a dream.

They have the courage to be judged, not only by that intimidating panel of nine people, but also by critics, their peers, and the world. They also have learned to face defeat. Some people imagine that falling down in front of an audience must be the worst moment in a skater's life. But we have our own code: We've been falling down since we were children and we know that when we fall, it means we've tried. To lose nerve, to back off, to chicken out is regarded by skaters a greater crime than sliding on our butts across the ice.

If Dean chooses to skate, he will experience the exhilaration we feel when we are on the ice. The freedom of playing with edges and turns, of learning to control our bodies so that we can lean on an edge as far as possible without wiping out, feels wonderful. Perfecting technique feels wonderful. Creating something from nothing feels wonderful. This is why the age-old argument of whether figure skating is a sport or an art is, to us, utterly irrelevant. As we live, our motivation changes. One day we may want to dance, another day to jump higher than anyone before us. Skating allows us to be individual.

Success comes in many forms. For a few it's winning a medal. For most, success is simply being able to go to the rink every day because we love to skate. It is forging strong friendships based on shared dreams, and traveling the world in pursuit of those dreams.

When I think back to my life in skating, I treasure all my memories, good and bad. If my little Dean grows up with a passion—any passion—then that will be my success, because the real dream is the journey.

Photographic references
are indicated in bold italics.

CREATED BY SANDRA BEZIC AND OPUS PRODUCTIONS INC.
PRODUCED BY OPUS PRODUCTIONS INC.

AUTHORS' NOTE

So many people have given their energy and their creativity toward making *The Passion to Skate* possible.

First, I thank my partner and husband, Dino, who has collaborated with me to conceive this book, influencing its creation with his wisdom and artistry. His love is my strength.

Thank you, David Hayes, for being my patient and positive teacher, my conscience, and for putting words to my instincts. He made the journey a treasured experience.

To capture that magical moment when a skater is in the perfect position with a perfect expression takes talent, dedication, and passion. Thank you to all the photographers who have mirrored skaters' souls, and especially thank you to Heinz Kluetmeier for his limitless generosity.

Sincerest thanks to: Nathalie Cook for making it a reality; Trisha Ricci for being my left hand; Jef Billings for his beautiful illustrations; Vilma Ricci for her encouragement; Kevin Albrecht for saying, "Your name is on it;" Marlon Brando for the wonderful dance.

Denise Benning-Reid, Peter Bregg, Craig Connaghan, Jilliaine Eicher, Mike Fanning, Tami Hahn, Martha Henderson, Kate Houze, Deborah Kagan, Linda Leaver, Mike Lobell, Elaine Mock, Ed Robinson, Michael and Nancy Rosenberg, Yuki Saegusa, Marguerite Schropp, Lydia Stephans, Segreda Tan, Cheryl Tate, Julie Vozick, Barb Wilson.

I am grateful to Derik Murray and Marthe Love and to the many people at Opus for their creativity and commitment to the vision.

To my parents, Dusan and Angeline, and my brother, Val, thank you isn't enough—it's in the genes.

To my patient little Dean—your joy has rekindled my own.

Finally to every skater I have ever shared the ice with, thank you for the inspiration.

SANDRA BEZIC

I would like to thank Sandra Bezic, who proved to be as talented and accommodating working with a writer on a blank sheet of paper as she is working with skaters on a blank sheet of ice. Our collaboration was a pleasure from beginning to end. I would also like to thank my literary agent, Jan Whitford, whose advice and efforts on my behalf are enormously valued, and Maya Gallus, for her constant creative and personal support.

DAVID HAYES

OPUS PRODUCTIONS INC.

President/Creative Director: DERIK MURRAY
Vice President, Production: DAVID COUNSELL
Design Director: DON BULL
Designer: GUYLAINE RONDEAU
Visual Coordinators: TRISHA RICCI, JOANNE POWERS
Photography Coordinator: COLETTE AUBIN

Chief Financial Officer: JAMIE ENGEN
General Counsel: RUTH CHANG
Marketing Manager: DAVID ATTARD
Sales Representative: CHRIS RICHARDSON
Office Manager: CATHERINE PALMER

Vice President/Publishing Director: MARTHE LOVE
Co-author: DAVID HAYES
Senior Editor: BRIAN SCRIVENER
Publishing Coordinator: JENNIFER LOVE
Publishing Associate: WENDY DARLING
Editorial Coordinator: MICHELLE HUNTER
Publishing Assistants: IRIS HO, ALLIE WILMINK
Proofreader: CATHERINE BENNETT

Opus Productions would like to extend a special thank you to:
SANDRA BEZIC, DINO RICCI, TRISHA RICCI, DEAN RICCI
International Management Group: NATHALIE COOK, CHERYL TATE

Turner Publishing Inc.: MICHAEL REAGAN, MICHAEL WALSH, KATHERINE BUTTLER, CAROLINE REAVES, MICHON WISE, JIM DAVIS

Opus Productions would like to acknowledge the following for their assistance and support:
STRUAN CAMPBELL SMITH, SHARYN DUFFY, MIKE FANNING (SCL IMAGING GROUP LTD.), MAYA GALLUS, THOM KLAUS, HEATHER MACAULAY, GLENN MCPHERSON, JOHN NICOLLS, PAULA WELLINGS, JAN WHITFORD

PHOTO CREDITS

Front cover: DINO RICCI/CRAIG CONNAGHAN, SCL IMAGING GROUP INC.
ALLSPORT/BOTTERILL, SHAUN: 91 left
ALLSPORT/BRUNSKILL, CLIVE: 45 below
ALLSPORT/BRUTY, SIMON: 74–75
ALLSPORT/CANNON, DAVID: 60 above left
ALLSPORT/CAZALS, MARCK: 66–67
ALLSPORT/COLE, CHRIS: 80 above
ALLSPORT/GUICHAOUA, YANN: 36 above, 106–7
ALLSPORT/MARTIN, BOB: 33, 82 left, 89
ALLSPORT/MARTIN, RICHARD: 34 below, 43 left, 54 left and right, 60 below left, 78–79, 83 above, 91 right, 96
ALLSPORT/POWELL, MIKE: 43 right, 82 below right, 99 left, back cover: top left
ALLSPORT/POWELL, STEVE: 28 right
ALLSPORT/VANDYSTADT, GÉRARD: ii, 36 below, 39 below, 54 middle, 55, 68, 82 above right, 135
ALLSPORT/WANT, ANTON: 80 below, 91 middle
BLAKE, MIKE: 58
BREGG, PETER/*Maclean's:* 86–87, 122 all, 124 both, 125 both, 126 all, 127 above right and left and below right
CBC/KRAYCHYK, GEORGE: 146 above
CBC/PHIPPS, FRED: 148 all, 149, 150 above, 152–53

CBC/STREET, DAVID: 147 left and below right
CHÂTAIGNEAU, GÉRARD: 103
COOKE, JERRY/*Sports Illustrated:* 61
CUDDINGTON, WAYNE/*Ottawa Citizen:* 46, 48, 49 both
ERSEK, IRENE: 102 left
EVON, MARC: 35 below, 57, 69, 77 both, 108, 112, 123, 157, 159 both
GRAINGER, GLENN/SCL IMAGING GROUP LTD.: back flap
GRANT, F. SCOTT: 41 left and above right
KLUETMEIER, HEINZ: 22 both, 154, 155, 163, 164, 166 both, 167, 168–69
KLUETMEIER, HEINZ/IMG: 64, 71, 81, 93 all, 95, 100 right, 101 right, 111 all, 113, 114 both, 115 both, 116, 119 both, 120 both, 121, 127 below left, 128–29, 160–61
KLUETMEIER, HEINZ/*Sports Illustrated:* 20, 23, 24, 25 right, 26, 29, 30–31, 35 above, 39 above
MACKSON, RICHARD/*Sports Illustrated:* 18–19, 25 left
MANNY MILLAN/*Sports Illustrated:* 25 middle, 27, 28 left, 44 right, 50–51, 52, 53
MARTIN, BOB/*Sports Illustrated:* 40 below
POTOPNYK, STEPHAN: 40 above, 41 below right, 70, 88, 94, 98, 109, 110, 156
POTOPNYK, STEPHAN/IMG: 34 above, 72

REID, PAUL: 65, 92, 99 right, 118
RICCI, DINO: 4, 6, 32, 44 left, 45 above, 60 right, 62, 84, 85, 104 above, 104 below, 105, 117 both, 130, 132 both, 133, 134 all, 137 all, 138, 139 all, 140, 141 all, 142 all, 143, 144, 145 all, 146 below, 150 below, 151, 170, 174, back cover: top right, below right, below left
SILVERSON, CAM: 97
STEPHANS, LYDIA: 131
VON TIEDEMANN, CYLLA: 83 below

COURTESY OF:

ANGELINE BEZIC: 2, 8, 9, 10, 11, 17 right
SANDRA BEZIC: 147 above right
BRIAN BOITANO: 12 below left
LU CHEN: 12 above left
PAUL MARTINI: 12 right
BARBARA UNDERHILL: 14, 17 left
KRISTI YAMAGUCHI: 15

FASHION DESIGNS:

BILLINGS, JEF: 100 left, 101 left, 102 right.